Praise for *microMARKETING*

"Greg presents the greatest hits of social media marketing, a litany of stories designed to persuade you to stop demanding the web conform to your desire for mass—and instead realize that mattering a lot to a few people is worth far more than mattering just a little to everyone."
—SETH GODIN, author of *Linchpin*

"Scale and media buying power are no longer a decisive advantage. As Greg Verdino shows with compelling examples of success, micro-MARKETING is big marketing. Now anybody can dominate a market. Especially *you*. So what are you waiting for?"
—DAVID MEERMAN SCOTT, bestselling author of *The New Rules of Marketing & PR*

"Greg Verdino makes the case for the death of mass marketing in a compelling way. Well written and loaded with interesting case histories."
—AL RIES, coauthor of *War in the Boardroom*

"In the creative marketing world, everyone is on a quest for the big idea. In what might seem like the ultimate paradox, Greg Verdino suggests that the best recipe for getting big results may actually require thinking *smaller*. *microMARKETING* offers a hopeful vision for anyone who has ever had to create a great marketing plan without a million-dollar budget or an army of resources. Yes, it *is* possible, and *microMARKETING* will show you how to do it."
—ROHIT BHARGAVA, author of *Personality Not Included* and SVP at Ogilvy 360 Digital Influence

"To paraphrase Kermit, it isn't easy being small. In *microMARKET-ING*, Greg Verdino has reeled in numerous examples of how big became passé and proves that in our overhyped society the teeniest push is the way in. Ironically, for a book that's all about the small, the examples have big consequences, and each story is told in an expressive manner. Verdino digs far beneath the surface (that's different), and practical lessons are proffered everywhere. Size queens beware: your days are numbered."
—RICHARD LAERMER, author of *2011: Trendspotting for the Next Decade* and CEO of RLM PR

"Filled with fresh strategies for engaging fragmented markets and frazzled customers."
—JILL KONRATH, bestselling author of *SNAP Selling* and *Selling to Big Companies*

"Greg Verdino's approach to micromarketing hits the nail on the head: social media efforts should put a face on the company and not focus on the tools. At Kodak, we strive to level the technology playing field by removing barriers and connecting people through social interaction, and we recognize that there is great power inherent in a single moment between a company and one of its customers—small is the new big. Micro is the new macro."

—THOMAS HOEHN, Director of Interactive Marketing at
Eastman Kodak Company

"We are in an evolutionary phase of marketing and going through a time when technology is increasingly becoming its backbone. What we've encountered over the past few years is tidily summed up in this book by the social media industry's bald uber-professor (yes, I mean Greg Verdino), and his vision about micro is spot on. If you are searching for the next big idea, you won't find it. We're entering an age of micromarketing where the next big idea is thousands of small ones. *microMARKETING* provides awesome articulation of this idea and is a must-read for anyone in marketing or technology."

—DARREN HERMAN, Chief Digital Media Officer at
kirshenbaum bond senecal + partners

"Verdino's thinking is anything but small. His insight will help businesses move from a fading era of mass marketing to embrace a meaningful genre of micro collaboration that builds macro markets."

—BRIAN SOLIS, author of *Engage* and
founder of BrianSolis.com

"All companies, regardless of size or market, struggle with the best way to capture the attention of their audience. Greg Verdino details how major brands have successfully done this by changing from mass marketing to micromarketing. He demonstrates that it is not about the tools you use, but what you do with them to create a personal experience. Follow Greg's seven shifts from mass to micro and you'll be a micromaven, capturing the attention of your audience, before you know it."

—DONNA M. TOCCI, Director of Web/New
Media at Ingersoll Rand

Get
Big Results
by Thinking
and Acting
Small

microMARKETING

GREG VERDINO

NEW YORK   CHICAGO   SAN FRANCISCO

LISBON   LONDON   MADRID   MEXICO CITY   MILAN

NEW DELHI   SAN JUAN   SEOUL   SINGAPORE

SYDNEY   TORONTO

The **McGraw·Hill** Companies

1 2 3 4 5 6 7 8 9 0   WFR/WFR   1 5 4 3 2 1 0

ISBN 978-0-07-166486-8
MHID   0-07-166486-6

Design by Lee Fukui and Mauna Eichner.

McGraw-Hill books are available at special quantity discounts to use as premiums and sales promotions, or for use in corporate training programs. To contact a representative, please visit the Contact Us pages at www.mhprofessional.com.

This book is printed on acid-free paper.

FOR MY FAVORITE SMALL THING AND MY BIGGEST RESULT: MY DAUGHTER, OLIVIA.

Contents

vii

Preface: From Small Beginnings ...

"The beginnings of all things are small."
— Marcus Tullius Cicero

"What if the real attraction of the Internet is not
its cutting-edge bells and whistles, its jazzy
interface, or any of the advanced technology
that underlies its pipes and wires? What if,
instead, the attraction is an atavistic
throwback to the prehistoric human
fascination with telling tales? In sharp contrast
to the alienation wrought by homogenized
broadcast media, sterilized mass "culture,"
and the enforced anonymity of bureaucratic
organizations, the Internet connected people to
each other and provided a space in which the
human voice would be rapidly rediscovered."
— The Cluetrain Manifesto

THE MASS MARKETER'S DILEMMA

Fifteen minutes into the meeting, and I already knew my client was heading down the wrong track. I had asked her to describe her ideal customer. After rattling off a litany of broadly defined demographic segments, squirming in her seat the entire time, she sheepishly blurted out, "Well, you know, basically we want to reach everyone."

I should provide some context before jumping into a bit of commentary and telling you a few things you should know before you start reading this book. I was in a conference room at the North American headquarters of a large global corporation that is a leader in its industry, seated across the table from a smart and seasoned brand manager responsible for driving hundreds of millions of dollars in revenue. Faced with my seemingly simple question, you might be tempted to respond the same way she did, prompting your agency to rise to the challenge with a "big idea" and a media plan that would "reach everyone" with prime-time television buys and Yahoo! home-page takeovers. But somewhere in the back of your mind, you'd probably already know that almost everyone you did reach would ignore your pleas for attention and that—in the end—you would most likely be disappointed with the results derived from the relatively few people who actually did take notice. During the pregnant pause that followed my client's expressed desire to reach everyone, I'm pretty sure this scenario was playing in her mind.

This is the mass marketer's dilemma: *you think big, you act big, and you spend big only to get results that are anything but.* Having spent more than a decade at large advertising, direct marketing, and digital agencies (where I worked with some of the world's biggest brands), I understand the mindset well, and believe me when I say that I'm not pointing fingers. At that time in my career, I would have fallen into the same trap myself. But for the past several years, I've been immersed in a very different, new marketing world. It is a world in which tweets can trump television, Facebook can get buyers fired-up better than newspaper FSIs, relationships speaks louder than radio, microinteractions can have more impact than microsites, and advocacy beats advertising for building brands.

I was coming from this perspective when I suggested to my client that I had some new ideas about how she might do things differently, market smarter, and deliver better results than she could expect from tried-but-no-longer-quite-so-true traditional approaches. With this book, I am suggesting the very same thing to you. It's time to embrace change and to do something (lots of things, actually) more in synch with the current state of society, the promise and potential of the social Web, and the current shape of the media landscape.

One of this book's key premises is that we are exiting—in fact, we most likely have already exited—the age in which mass mattered. We now do business in an age when it is far better to be everything to the right someone than it is to attempt to offer something for everyone, but this requires us to change the way we think, act, and go to market if we hope to achieve the results we can no longer expect from faltering traditional approaches. This book is about making the shift from mass marketing to micromarketing, and in it I hope to provide you with ideas and inspiration on the one hand, and practical guidelines and actionable approaches on the other. I hope to convince you that thinking and acting small have become the best ways to achieve big results.

microMARKETING IS NOT THE NEXT BIG THING

This book is about change—the ways in which consumers have changed, the ways in which technology and media have changed, some of the ways in which marketing *must* change if marketers hope to catch up and succeed—but it isn't really about the next big thing at all. I would argue that the very notion of a next big thing is as outdated as the traditional interruption-oriented marketing approaches so many (frankly, far too many) marketers still count on—with diminishing results—to promote their businesses. In many ways, micromarketing is a back-to-basics approach to engaging people and sharing stories more effectively in a world that is decidedly different than it was 50 years ago when mass production and mass media combined to offer a potent one-two punch. A world that is decidedly different than it was even 15 years ago, before most of us had easy access to the World Wide Web. But interestingly enough, a world *not* so different than it was 150 years ago when the local shopkeeper knew every customer's name and preferences, people mostly purchased the goods they needed from people they knew personally, and positive peer-to-peer recommendations—often derived as much from positive interactions with the people at a business as from the quality of the purchased product itself—served as one of the few marketing vehicles available to most business owners. Fortunately, it was also one of the most effective . . . and it still is.

This is probably a good time to acknowledge that the term *micromarketing* itself isn't new either, although what I mean when I use it is. According to Wikipedia, the term micromarketing was "coined in 1988, by Ross Nelson Kay, as a . . . form of target marketing that was more precise and focused than typical niche marketing techniques. Micromarketing became functionally viable with the proliferation of affordable home computers . . . [and] remains the most effective technique for small business users to sustain, build and grow their own brand." But I should also point out that—while most of Kay's original definition remains relevant and has, in fact, informed my thinking—this book is not about *your former CMO's micromarketing*. I am writing about micromarketing for a new age, a series of approaches infused to their core with a social media sensibility, powered by social computing technologies, and optimized to allow businesses of all sizes and types to thrive in a landscape transformed by three key trends:

→ The proliferation of *microcultures*

→ The explosion in *microcontent*

→ And the emergence of influential *micromavens* that can often play a key role in making or breaking a brand.

SPEAKING OF MICROMAVENS: TAKING INSPIRATION FROM UNLIKELY SOURCES

If we're being totally honest with ourselves, we must admit that corporations are late to the game; when most do finally arrive, they often read from an out-of-date playbook or play by the wrong rules altogether. While I certainly present more than a few business cases throughout the book and by no means wish to discount the good work that companies like Best Buy, Coca-Cola, and Ford, among others, are doing in social media and (even if they don't yet use the term) micromarketing, I firmly believe that marketers can learn more by observing what individuals are doing (and accomplishing) with social approaches, platforms, tools, and technologies.

You will meet a lone dancer, a masked magician, a cancer survivor, a science fiction author, a makeup artist, and a handful of other regular people who exhibit the essence of micromarketing in ways that elude most trained businesspeople. In telling their stories, I have done my best to draw out a series of insights about what makes these people and their projects tick. I have aimed to impart a set of approaches I believe even the biggest businesses can apply to get it right and get results without investing so heavily in tired, traditional approaches that don't deliver as well as they once did. If ever you find yourself reading along and thinking *interesting, but what does this have to do with me*, read on. The answer is bound to be: *everything*.

TWITTER, TWITTER, TWITTER: A FEW WORDS ABOUT TECHNOLOGY

Building upon my previous point, people are at the heart of every story I recount in this book, just as people—and not the technologies we use—are at the heart of the social media revolution that has laid the foundation for my micromarketing philosophy.

Granted, technology in general and the social Web in particular
appear in supporting roles in each and every tale. The struggles,
triumphs, defeats, and simple moments of honest human-to-
human interaction I describe throughout this book play out
against a backdrop built from bits and bytes. Much of the action
takes place on Facebook and YouTube, Flickr and Twitter, and a
host of other social media platforms du jour. Yet this is not a
how-to book: you won't learn tips and tricks for setting up your
Facebook Page, building your blog, crafting the perfect 140-
character tweet, or shooting that one unlikely video that will
enter the ranks of the Web's most watched content. I believe that—
given the rate of change—spelling out today's best practices for
tomorrow's readers often turns out to be a fool's errand. And waiting for those best practices to become widely accepted within the
industry is a business person's surefire plan for getting left behind.

I can also tell you that writing a book about social technology is hard. Twitter was arguably everybody's darling as I *wrote*
these words (Marsha Brady to the rest of the Web's Jan), but it
might not be by the time you *read* them. Mobile social software
start-ups like Foursquare and Gowalla are stealing some of
Twitter's thunder and may prove to offer more for marketers
over time. Both garner a few mentions in the book, but neither
feature prominently in any of the case studies. Even as I made
the final edits to my manuscript, Apple introduced its highly
anticipated iPad; Facebook announced an aggressive push
toward an open graph that will allow content creators to make
virtually any site or asset social; WordPress developers introduced innovations that could turn any blog running on its publishing platform into a ready-made social network. Given the
timing of these developments (and countless others), I couldn't

possibly have worked these in, even though all of them are likely to have massive implications for marketers (micro or otherwise). My advice to you is this: if you focus less on the technologies and more on the takeaways, you'll get more out of this book.

Don't get me wrong. These stories are timely (or as timely as they can be given the publishing process), but I'd like to think the lessons they impart are timeless or will at least remain relevant long after today's social computing giants give way to the next generation of Web technologies. In other words: the examples I use are tangible and specific, and (*yes*) sites like Twitter, Facebook, and YouTube seem to be recurring players. But the ideas, approaches, and guiding principles that underlie the examples can just as easily be applied to whatever platforms come next. For better or worse, our business is never short on shiny objects, but good ideas should prevail long after the *next new thing* has lost its luster.

A FEW MORE WORDS ABOUT TECHNOLOGY: MAKING THE MOST OF THIS BOOK

Given the themes I cover in the pages ahead—among them the idea that content's basic building blocks have become smaller and more easily shared over the course of the past decade, the notion that both the audiences and their attention spans have been splintered into ever-smaller slices, and the increased importance of small-scale interactions and real-time engagement—it is perhaps somewhat ironic that I've chosen to present them in such a traditional format. With this in mind, I've done my best to apply at least some of the principles I preach by giving you a few important ways to interact with the content, to access supplemental materials that help bring the stories and case studies to life, and to facilitate connections and conversations about micromarketing.

Throughout the text, you will see call-outs that point you to the Websites, blogs, Twitter profiles, videos, photos, and other content I'm writing about. I'd like to encourage you to read with the book in one hand and your mouse in the other. And if you find something particularly interesting, insightful, or inspirational and you choose to share it—on Twitter for example (you are on Twitter already, aren't you?)—you might want to use the hashtag *#micromktg* to help your connections understand where you're coming from. And to help me understand how microchunked content in and about this book finds its way into the stream and benefits from the network effect. Don't worry; if you have no idea what most of that meant, you will by the time you finish the book.

SO WHAT DO *YOU* THINK?

Are you ready to learn more? Allow me to make one last point before we get started.

As Malcolm Gladwell writes in the introduction to his collection of essays, *What the Dog Saw*, "Good writing does not succeed or fail on the strength of its ability to persuade ... It succeeds or fails on the strength of its ability to engage you, to make you think, to give you a glimpse into someone else's head—even if in the end you conclude that someone else's head is not a place you'd really like to be."

I hope the stories I tell, the cases I make, and the arguments I present will persuade you to try something new and different the next time you face your own marketing challenges. But it's not really my place to try and convince you that I'm right. In fact, I will be the first to admit I don't know all the answers—although I do think I'm on the right track. Like Gladwell, I'd rather entertain and engage you while you have this book open (or powered up), provide you with a glimpse into how I think about marketing in a post–mass media age, and make you think after you've read the last word.

That said, you'll find lots of my own thinking in the pages ahead. In the first two chapters alone, I provide my perspectives on how media, technology, and society have changed over the past several years; highlight seven irreversible shifts affecting marketers today; and explain why and how I believe brands must begin thinking and acting small if they hope to remain relevant to consumers. Then in Chapters 3 through 9, I offer deep dives into each of the seven shifts and, using real-world examples as a foundation, articulate a variety of new approaches that form the basis of a successful micromarketing strategy.

In the final chapter though, I offer you the opportunity to collect your thoughts and begin applying *my* ideas to *your* business. As you do that—and in fact, as you read the book as a whole—you should feel free to reach out to me with questions, comments, ideas, arguments, and your own examples of micromarketing at work. At the end of Chapter 9 you will find a comprehensive list of ways to do just that. In the meantime, you can begin by visiting the book's Website (**micromarketingbook.com**), joining its Facebook community (**facebook.com/micromarketing**), or connecting with me on Twitter (**@gregverdino** and **@micromktg**). And of course, you can always e-mail me at **greg.verdino@powered .com** or strike up a conversation at **www.gregverdino.com**.

Acknowledgments

I've often heard it said that writing a book is a solitary experience, but looking back at the process that led to the publication of the volume you hold in your hands today, it seems like nothing could be further from the truth. I would like to take this opportunity to recognize some of the people who have in some way shaped my thinking, influenced my work, helped me out, or stood by my side. There isn't room to list everybody, my memory isn't what it used to be, and you wouldn't want to read a dozen pages' worth of other people's names—so if you think your name should appear below but can't seem to find it listed, rest assured I'll make room for you next time around.

I would like to begin by thanking the *crayonistas*—in particular Joseph Jaffe, Jane Quigley, and "Rock Me" Amadeo Plaza—for their friendship, support, hard work, and inspiration over the course of the past few years. And thanks to my new Powered, Inc., colleagues including Ken Nicolson, Aaron Strout, Kathy Warren, Natanya Anderson, Ron Green, and David Settle—plus Kevin Tate and Greg Rau at StepChange Group and Steve Kleinberg and Jen van der Meer of Drillteam Marketing—for helping *the company formerly known as crayon* take our business to the next level.

Thank you to Donya Dickerson, Ron Martirano, and the rest of the McGraw-Hill team for their belief *in* me and commitment *to* me, even after my best attempts to avoid submitting the original proposal and in the face of at least a few subsequent missed deadlines. Thanks also to my agent Ethan Friedman of LevelFiveMedia for his invaluable advice and much-needed assistance throughout the entire writing and publishing process.

A special thanks to Anthony Perez. Without his tireless effort, attention to detail, expert research skills, and smart thinking (not to mention his abilities to juggle multiple jobs and pull all-nighters), entire chunks of this book would have remained unwritten. I'm fairly certain his work has made me look smarter than I am. If you're reading along and think, "Wow, I didn't know that," *you* may want to thank Anthony as well. You can tweet your thanks to @brandthony if you're so inclined.

I am grateful for my friends, fans, followers, subscribers, and connections—everyone who has read my blog over the past few years, the people I've had the pleasure of interacting with in the social media sphere, and the *real worlders* I've had the opportunity to meet in person at tweetups, meetups, conferences, and other social media events. Some of the ideas presented in this book have appeared on my blog or in presentations I have given, usually in one half-baked form or another. Feedback from my community has helped make those ideas better, and there's a little bit of everyone else's good thinking in each chapter of this book.

While we're on the subject of good thinking, I am grateful for every blogger, podcaster, content creator, and *twit(terer)* that has inspired me with his or her own thought leadership. They are the micromavens that have earned my attention. Although there are too many to list them all by name, you might check out the *Advertising Age* Power 150 or the tables of contents in Drew McLellan and Gavin Heaton's *Age of Conversation* crowd-sourced social media anthologies for starters.

Beyond the blogosphere, I would like to acknowledge a long but necessarily incomplete list of big thinkers who have inspired my own *small* thinking: Chris Anderson, Paul Arden, James Carse, Douglas Coupland, Stephen J. Dubner and Steven D. Levitt, Bob Garfield, William Gibson, Malcolm Gladwell, Seth Godin, Umair Haque, Chip and Dan Heath, Jackie Huba and Ben McConnell, Henry Jenkins, Lawrence Lessig, Grant McCracken, Marshall McLuhan, Marty Neumeier, Douglas Rushkoff, Barry Schwartz, David Meerman Scott, Clay Shirky, James Surowiecki, Mike Walsh, Bill Wasik, David Weinberger, and Larry Winget. Their influence may not always be obvious, and to be frank, I don't always agree with their points of view, but my shelves are better with their books upon them, and my opinions about business, marketing, and sometimes the world are more informed for having read them.

I would be remiss if I didn't give thanks to my parents for raising me right and my teachers for *learnin'* me how to write.

If it weren't for the former, I wouldn't be here, and if it weren't for the latter, these words wouldn't be here (at least not in the proper order, and certainly without at least occasionally accurate spelling, grammar, and punctuation).

Last, not least, and most of all: *thank you, thank you, thank you, Amanda.* You have spent far too much time staring at my back as I sat hunched over my laptop, you suffered through the first draft of my manuscript before I showed it to anyone else, and you never once faltered in your love, friendship, advice, encouragement, support, patience, kisses, cuddles, and belief. You are my happiness, the love of my life, and my favorite nerd. I love you forever, bunny.

Disclosures

If the marketing industry is small, the social media community is smaller. Because I earn my living in the former and live, document, and mediate so much of my life through the latter, it is inevitable that this work contains some conflicts of interest. Many of the people and companies mentioned in this book are now—or have at some point during my career been—clients, colleagues, friends, or foes. I hope to count the rest of the people among my friends or colleagues, and the rest of the companies among my clients at some point in the future. The foes will take care of themselves.

Where I've written about a marketing program—or even a client—that my company or I have been involved with directly, I have done my best to clearly disclose that fact either in the text itself or in a footnote. That said, my opinions are my own, *micro-MARKETING* is not a sponsored conversation, and no small animals were harmed during the writing of this book.

1

The Next Big Thing Is Lots and Lots of Small Things

The Future of Marketing Is Micro

"The rules of the finite game may not change; the rules of an infinite game *must* change. Finite players play within boundaries; infinite players play *with* boundaries. Finite players are serious; infinite games are playful. A finite player plays to be powerful; an infinite player plays with strength. A finite player consumes time; an infinite player generates time. The finite player aims for eternal life; the infinite player aims for eternal birth. *The choice is yours.*"

—James P. Carse

UNSTOPPABLE

On a sloped hillside in Washington State's Columbia River Gorge, Collin Wynter started dancing a vaguely offbeat, loose-limbed shuffle to the distant sound of Santigold's "Unstoppable." This isn't as odd as it sounds. Collin was just one of thousands of attendees at Sasquatch! 2009, a three-day music festival featuring dozens of performers ranging from obscure up-and-comers to the biggest names in alternative rock. You might have expected plenty of dancing; you would have been wrong.

In Collin's corner of the canyon, he was the *only* person dancing as Santigold performed on the Gorge Amphitheater stage far below.

Hundreds of spectators dotted the hill around him. Exhibiting little if any inclination to join in the fun, most were seated and were seemingly giving Collin wide berth to perform his one-man show. I imagine some of the onlookers were amused, others uncomfortable with Collin's unself-conscious display. At least a few must have considered the scene worth capturing on film, because in the days following the festival a number of shaky camcorder videos of Collin found their way onto YouTube. Though these amateur videographers might have aimed to do nothing more than entertain their friends by sharing an awkward moment of public abandon, they actually documented something much more interesting than that. What happened in the few minutes after the cameras started rolling would turn Collin Wynter into a bona fide microcelebrity and provide one of the citizen cameramen—a 20-something using the YouTube handle *dkellerm*—with his first and, as of this writing, only viral video hit.

Uploaded on May 26, 2009, dkellerm's video begins with footage of Collin Wynter dancing alone. After around 20 seconds though, a second man ambles into the frame and begins dancing, followed by another half a minute later. By the minute-and-a-half mark, Collin has been joined by a small group—and that's when the video really gets interesting. From that moment on, dancer after dancer joins the fray, many literally *running* to get in on the action before the song ends. By the end of the three-minute video, hundreds of young men and women fill the frame, dancing alongside Collin in an impromptu hillside dance party.

Watch the Sasquatch Dancing Man on YouTube
bit.ly/dancingmanvideo

Seen at face value, dkellerm's video seems to document something quite trivial, nothing more than a mildly entertaining moment in time. But by a more generous interpretation, it could be said to portray a human story with universal appeal. It is about leaders and followers, about risk takers and the risk averse, about some people's desire to stand apart from the crowd and other people's drive to be part of something bigger than themselves. In some small way, it's about the ways in which people connect with one another and share experiences.

Viewed through a marketer's lens, the video dramatizes the consumer-to-consumer viral effect that brands often hope to achieve and plays it out before our eyes over the course of three short minutes. As the scene shifts from individual action to group behavior to the movement of the crowd, we see a clear illustration of the dynamics between the influencer—several influencers actually, if you consider not only Collin himself but the second and third dancers—and the influenced.

And so within mere weeks of its initial upload, this particular video had garnered more than 1 million YouTube views, fueled by word of mouth, attention from dozens of bloggers who embedded the clip on their sites, and a community of consumers who shared the link by e-mail and instant message and across social networking sites like Facebook and Twitter. In that same time period, several similar YouTube videos capturing the same few minutes from Sasquatch! had each amassed hundreds of thousands of additional views, bringing the total audience within range for a respectable cable television show rating. As often happens on the heels of viral video success, the mainstream media—in this case, some of the largest news outlets in Collin's native country of Canada—picked up the story and featured the video in reports about the Web phenomenon he had sparked.

The band performances at the Sasquatch! Festival got the obligatory coverage from the music press, but for more than a month after the last band's final note, the Internet was abuzz with chatter about the "Sasquatch Dancing Man," as Collin was dubbed by video watchers when he was just an anonymous dancer who, by simply moving to his own groove, started a movement.

Yet by the time you read this, the odds are good that just about everyone will have forgotten all about him. But don't worry. There were thousands of Web video successes before Collin Wynter, and there are thousands more waiting in the wings, poised to take the stage and provide a few moments of offbeat entertainment.

THE REVOLUTION WAS NOT TELEVISED

While Collin Wynter was still basking in the glow of his new-found short-lived Internet stardom, a very different movement of far greater importance—a revolution, in fact—was breaking out halfway across the globe.

On June 12, 2009, Iranians went to the polls to vote for their next president, resulting in a surprising 2-to-1 landslide victory by the incumbent Mahmoud Ahmadinejad over popular challenger Mir Hossein Moussavi. Fueled by claims of election fraud and other abuses, thousands of Moussavi's supporters took to the streets in a series of protests that quickly escalated into widespread riots, both in the city of Tehran and throughout the country. As the violence escalated over the next couple of days, Iranian authorities clamped down on local access to mainstream media outlets and major Internet sites (including social networking giant Facebook) in an effort to limit the protesters' ability to organize and get up-to-the-minute information, and the authorities also banned foreign journalists to prevent the international spread of news about the highly charged situation.

But clearly the government hadn't anticipated the ease with which the population would overcome the information lockdown. Armed with handheld devices capable of transmitting text messages and capturing everything from still photographs to video clips, empowered by friction-free social media distribution networks, Iranian citizens began delivering a torrent of real-time updates to interested, supportive, and hyperconnected Web users around the globe. Despite the crackdown on mainstream media reporting and consumption, the flow of information was—literally—unstoppable.

Over the coming days, hundreds of thousands of short-form messages were transmitted over Twitter, containing everything from rallying cries to minute-by-minute reports from people actively participating in the protests. Follow-up tweets from Twitter users outside Iran, spreading the word and pledging support, drove the number of messages into the millions. Widespread use of the hashtag (a semantic device that renders Twitter content on a given topic easier to find, filter, and aggregate) #iranelection turned a disjointed series of isolated exclamations into a unified, living record of political unrest.

Elsewhere on the Internet, Iranian bloggers compiled their own records of the strife happening outside their homes. At a time when no print or broadcast journalist had the means to report the news, small local blogs like Revolutionary Road used a hodgepodge of text, photos, and videos to deliver a dynamic, near-real-time window into the riots. Thousands upon thousands of photographs and grainy minute-long videos, shot by hundreds of Iranian citizens, found their way onto content-sharing sites like Flickr and YouTube.

Read the Revolutionary Road Blog

bit.ly/iranprotests

Despite the Iranian government's efforts to quell the spread of information, the story of Iran's politically charged revolution was being told word by word, image by image, minute by minute, *as it happened*, entirely from the perspectives of individual people living through this crisis.

The resulting stream of nibble-sized items—assuming you had the patience to piece it all together—was raw, unfiltered, emotional, largely anonymous, and (let's face facts) more than a little bit unreliable. It was also an undeniably authentic, uniquely captivating record that documented a historic world event in a wholly new way that would have been impossible (if not unimaginable) just a few years before.

Whereas a single tweet, image, or video—or even a steady stream of updates from a sole user—might have ultimately been less than significant, the accumulated output of hundreds of people took on a remarkable heft. And so the rest of the world didn't watch the story unfold on their television screens, filtered by professional news agencies and served up in well-produced packages of facts, context, and commentary. Using Google, RSS feeds, and Twitter searches, paying particular attention to the information their personal networks found noteworthy enough to spread through their own Twitter profiles, social network updates, and blogs, people became their own news agencies, aggregators, curators, storytellers, and distribution channels as the crisis played out before them across a hyperfragmented, hyperdistributed social media landscape.

As if this all were not remarkable enough, one final development underscores the degree to which this event was not only an important moment in world history but also a pivotal moment in the history of media communications. It's probably not an understatement to say that with #iranelection we saw a major shift in how the news is reported and consumed. And it is a change that is no less significant than the shifts from reading tomorrow morning's newspaper to watching this evening's television news, and from watching this evening's television news to keeping an eye on breaking stories presented on 24-hour cable news networks.

Starved of their own original source material and, by this point, woefully out of step, the mainstream media outlets turned to the social media maelstrom of tweets, posts, images, and clips as inspiration for their own secondhand coverage of the Iranian revolution. Venerable old media institutions like the *New York Times* and the *Atlantic Monthly*[1] harvested bits of news directly from the social media stream, curating the first-person feeds, adding a layer of context and commentary for their Web readers. Broadcast and cable news reports regularly featured shaky camera-phone videos culled from YouTube, Facebook, and video blogs.

Sasquatch Dancing Man is just one small instance of short-lived Internet celebrity, a single case of a human-scale story that grew to Web-scale proportions through simple (albeit digitally enabled) word of mouth, and proof that just about anyone armed with a means of creating and distributing content can attract an audience. But #iranelection represents a game-changing moment when the eyes of the world—and significantly, the eyes of the world's preeminent mass media producers—were trained on "the people formerly known as the audience."[2]

At first glance, these two very different stories may not seem to have many things in common. But they do. Both are examples of a radically changed media landscape, highlight the technologies that play a central role in driving the change, and of course illustrate significant shifts in consumer behaviors and media preferences. Both speak to the new nature of content creation and distribution. Each in its own way demonstrates how we are moving—I might argue, *have already moved*—beyond the era of centralized, top-down, command-and-control mass communications.

Now, I'm well aware that I'm not the first person to propose that we're moving beyond the era of mass communications, and this isn't meant to be just another book about the death of big media or the end of advertising. Multibillion-dollar industries don't disappear overnight. But it would be naïve to ignore the fact that the rules have changed and that, to get the results we need in order to survive and thrive in a post–mass media age, the way we market must—not might or should, but *must*—change along with them. Simply put: mass isn't nearly as mass *as it once was*, the things we've long taken for granted no longer work as well *as they once did*, and in a variety of ways the real action seems to have shifted from the center to the edges.

I assume you've heard this all before—I'd be shocked if you haven't—but I think it's worth looking back before we look forward.

BEHOLD THE MILLION-CHANNEL FUTURE
(FRAGMENTATION NOT INCLUDED)

If you're old enough to remember a media universe dominated by ABC, CBS, and NBC, the first time you heard the statement "I want my MTV," and the high-pitched squeal of a 300-baud modem, then the odds are good you'll also remember the first time you heard talk of the coming million-channel universe.

For me it was back in the early 1990s, when dial-up services from America Online, Prodigy, and CompuServe dominated the newly minted consumer Internet and the number of television networks available on even the most robust cable system was pretty limited by today's standards. I was a media planner at the direct marketing agency Wunderman Cato Johnson* when, one afternoon, the media director ushered our entire department into a well-appointed conference room for a lunchtime presentation about "the next big thing." (His words, not mine, and oh, if I had a dime for every time I've heard those words over the course of my career ...)

Inside that conference room, a small team of presenters fed us sandwiches and regaled us with visions of a "million-channel future" in which consumers would access thousands upon thousands of rich interactive content channels and use their remote controls to click away at targeted, immersive advertising. I remember leaving that conference excited about the future of mass media, imagining all the opportunities presented by more impactful ad units running on tomorrow's television screens.

---

* Wunderman Cato Johnson is now simply Wunderman, and the U.S. media department has been merged into WPP Group's MEC Global.

FRAGMENTATION IS THE NEW NORMAL

Fast-forward nearly 20 years, and I suppose you might say the presenters' vision was half right. We got our million-channel universe, but it doesn't look like the love child of CBS and CompuServe that promised to keep us glued to the tube en masse, clicking on interactive ads. In fact, we didn't get here through an evolution of the mass media we knew, but through a revolution staged outside the walls of the mass media firmament. And as any marketer struggling to break through the clutter or grappling with the reality of a sub-1 percent response rate knows, the arrival of the million-channel universe didn't make traditional advertising *more* effective at capturing consumers' attention; it made it *less so*.

You know this better than I do: if you are a dyed-in-the-wool mass marketer, fragmentation is not your friend. In his 2005 book *Life After the 30-Second Spot*, my colleague Joseph Jaffe debunks the very notion of mass reach. "The continued fragmentation and proliferation of media touch points and content alternatives makes reaching masses of audiences difficult and aggregating them even more difficult ... the only mass that is present these days is mass confusion, distraction, and clutter."

But as Chris Anderson observed a year later in *The Long Tail*, the shift away from mass isn't just a matter of channels and choices, mass confusion and media clutter. It's a matter of *culture*. In Anderson's view:

> [The] Long Tail forces and technologies that are leading to
> an explosion of variety and abundant choice in the content
> we consume are also tending to lead us into tribal eddies.

When mass culture breaks apart, it doesn't re-form into a different mass. Instead, it turns into millions of microcultures, which coexist and interact in a baffling array of ways ... In short, we're seeing a shift from mass culture to *massively parallel culture* ... we're leaving the watercooler era, when most of us listened, watched, and read from the same, relatively small pool of mostly hit content. And we're entering the microculture era, when we're all into different things.

And when we're all into different things, it's only natural that a wholly new, massively parallel universe of content creators should emerge to satisfy the hyperniche interests of our millions of microcultures.

Enter the age of *microcontent* ...

MICROCONTENT AND THE INFINITE CHANNEL PRESENT

To be clear, even the concept of microcontent has been with us almost as long as the Web itself. But in the post–Web 2.0 era—ripe with tweets and Facebook status updates, noisy with FriendFeed conversations, and populated with Posterous *lifestreams*—it is clearly an idea whose time has come, even if most mass media outlets (and the many companies that rely upon mass marketing approaches) wish it were otherwise.

Web usability guru Jakob Nielsen wrote about microcontent as early as 1998 in reference to small, easily digestible bits of information that represent larger pieces of macrocontent—the headline to the complete article, the subject line to the body of an e-mail, the page title that appears in a Google search result to the content of the page the search result links to. By 2002, blogging pioneer Anil Dash built upon Nielsen's notion of microcontent by adding the critical characteristic of portability. Dash's micro-content wasn't just small; it was created with multiple platforms in mind, allowing audiences to access it via RSS feed readers, e-mail programs, Web browsers, or handheld devices.

By the time media analyst Umair Haque turned his attention to the phenomenon in 2005, the social Web was already begin-ning to gain traction with mainstream consumers and attract the attention of the most forward-looking marketing minds. The social media implications already evident in Dash's definition became a clear distinguishing characteristic in Haque's. Coining the terms *Media 2.0* and *micromedia*, Haque described a new media landscape that was markedly different from the tradi-tional mass media environment. His new media landscape was by definition social, and content was broken down to its core components and primed not only for consumption but also for curation, aggregation, distribution, and manipulation. In Haque's words:

> What is micromedia? Micromedia is media produced by prosumers (or amateurs; sometimes, it's called "consumer-generated content"). Micromedia differs fundamentally from mass media ... it's usually microchunked ... Consider blogs. Their microchunking into posts is frictionless; light-weight standards like HTML and RSS coordinate it. This makes blogs plastic: posts can be cheaply linked to, syndi-cated, remixed, or otherwise filtered and tweaked. The

open-access platforms that bloggers use to produce blogs also allow others to contribute complements, like comments, tags, and ratings; making micromedia liquid. Other kinds of services can then access, aggregate, and filter this micromedia, and, for example, individualize streams of content for communities or individual consumers.[3]

The result? Not a well-ordered and ultimately finite million-channel landscape, but a rough-and-ready *infinite microchannel playground* where an obscenely large, always growing storehouse of bite-sized chunks of microcontent—representing every aesthetic from professional to prosumer to personal—gets produced, presented, combined, ripped apart, and recombined in a virtually unlimited number of ways. Any attempt to quantify the order of magnitude here stifles the mind. Consider just a handful of representative data points:*

➡ According to Nielsen BlogPulse, there are more than 126 million blogs and bloggers publish more than 1 million new posts every day.

➡ While there has been plenty of debate over how many people actually use Twitter on an ongoing basis (although by any count the number is in the double-digit millions), there is no disputing the fact that the active *Twitterati* post more than 50 million tweets on an average day. That's more than 600 tweets per second. Interesting from the

---

* Given the dynamic state of the social Web, the numbers that follow will be out of date by the time you read them, but they are still a good gauge of the sheer scale of the explosion in microcontent creation and consumption.

standpoint of peer-to-peer distribution, nearly *20 percent* of those tweets contain links to other Websites or pieces of online content.

➡ Wikipedia, the free online encyclopedia, has more than 91,000 active writers who contribute to the composition of more than 15 million articles in 270 different languages.

➡ Flickr users have uploaded more than 4 billion photos to Yahoo!'s popular image-sharing service.

➡ YouTube houses more than 70 million videos, uploaded by more than 200,000 different publishers (some professional, many not). And if you're looking for a tangible example of the microchunking of entertainment, you might note that the average clip runs just 2 minutes and 46 seconds from start to finish.

➡ If that's not already enough video content to keep you entertained for several lifetimes, YouTube members add 24 hours of new video content each and every minute.

➡ There's certainly an audience for all this video because, according to research published by TechCrunch, YouTube's audience may view as many as 1.2 billion videos per day.

➡ Of course, YouTube is only one of many online video sites; according to comScore MediaMetrix, it captures just a 26 percent share of total online viewing. Across all video sites, the average viewer watches 187 clips in any given month.

⇒ Facebook members share more than 5 billion pieces of content each week, ranging from Web links, news stories, notes, and blog posts to photos and videos. And yes, that really is billion with a *b*.

⇒ When a Facebook member wants to add additional networking functionality, express herself, entertain her friends, or even declare loyalty for a favorite brand, she can choose from among 500,000 different third-party applications.

⇒ Of course, apps aren't a Facebook phenomenon alone. For mobile consumers, the Apple iPhone App Store offers more than 159,000 applications from more than 32,000 independent publishers; and as of April 2009, the App Store had served more than 4 billion (yup, with a *b* again) downloads.

Clearly, we're talking about lots and lots of small things ("loosely joined," to paraphrase *The Cluetrain Manifesto* coauthor David Weinberger[4]), and this profoundly changes not only the face of media, but the way companies must market through media.

DUDE, WHERE'S MY CAMERA?

Now is probably a good time to point out that the news is not all bad. You might even say that where hyperfragmentation and the microcontent explosion are potential busts for big media and mass marketers, they are boons for consumers in Chris

Anderson's microculture scenario. In fact, if you buy into the long tail theory, microculture and microcontent go hand in hand, forming either a vicious circle or a virtuous cycle depending on your point of view.

As much as it stretches our attention span and taxes our patience as marketers, the massive explosion in media alternatives makes it possible for splintered audiences to find and consume precisely the content they want, when and where they want it. Or as News Corporation chief Rupert Murdoch—if there's a more suitable spokesperson for mass media's old guard, I don't know who it might be—said in a July 2006 *Wired* interview, "Technology is shifting the power away from the editors, the publishers, the establishment, the media elite. Now it's the people who are in control."

More recently and with less fanfare, actor Ashton Kutcher—an early celebrity proponent of Twitter and other social tools—channeled Murdoch and articulated the magnitude of this shift in a Webcam-style video he uploaded to YouTube in mid-2009:

> For one person to actually have the ability to broadcast to as many people as a major media network, I think sort of signifies the turning of the tide from traditional news outlets to social news outlets. With our video cameras on our cell phones and our picture cams and our blogging and our Twittering and our posting and our Facebooking, we actually become the source of the news, and the broadcasters of the news, and the consumers of the news so I think that that's kind of a significant thing . . . that we actually have the ability to turn the tide where social media and social news

outlets can become as powerful as the major news outlets . . . it's sort of power to the people and I like that a lot.

Watch Ashton Kutcher's Video on YouTube

bit.ly/kutchersays

Put aside the facts that Kutcher is hardly a regular person and Murdoch—not you, me, or Johnny down the block—is still, in every sense of the word, very much *in control* at News Corp (and probably not as big a fan of the disruptive powers of the Web as he might have seemed in that *Wired* interview; as I write this, he is striking a blow against "the people who are in control" in an effort to convert his newspaper Websites to a paid subscription model). The point is absolutely spot-on. The big shift in the media landscape isn't just about how we consume; it's about what we create. In the microcontent age, every person is a media mogul (no matter how small). And this brings us back to the Sasquatch Dancing Man and #iranelection.

Even less than a decade ago, dkellerm might have left Sasquatch! with an amusing story to tell and, perhaps, shared that story with a roomful of friends. The citizens of Tehran may have documented their personal experiences during the postelection riots, but when the rest of the world tuned into the day's news reports, we would have gotten detailed accounts of events transpiring everywhere *except* Iran. After all, people have always been fond of telling one another stories, of sharing even the minutest details—and certainly the most monumental moments—of their lives with the people around them. But over the course of the past decade, technology has made it easier than ever to share our lives with scores of people around the world.

A growing majority of so-called regular people have access to low-cost, increasingly powerful content-creation devices that are small enough to fit in the palms of their hands or the pockets of their pants. Handheld video camcorders, pocket-sized digital cameras, and photo/video-capable mobile phones have become nearly ubiquitous and have significantly lowered the historical barriers for anyone to document the people, places, and events in *their world*—and share them with *the world*. At the same time, free and open access to democratized channels of distribution— from social networking tools like Facebook, Twitter, YouTube, and Flickr, to publishing systems as diverse as iTunes and the WordPress blogging platform—makes it possible for just about anyone with Internet access to reach a mass audience almost as easily as NBC or the *New York Times* can. Technology has leveled the playing field, if not slanted it in favor of the individual, as was the case with #iranelection.

FROM MASS MARKETING TO microMARKETING

I'm usually the first person to point out that it's important to look at the big picture, to focus on the trends rather than the tools. Even so, it's easy to get lost in the sheer magnitude of what we see happening across the Web today, to focus a bit *too much* on the size of the blogosphere, YouTube's scale, Facebook's total membership, or Twitter's meteoric rise. When viewed this way, any one of these platforms—not to mention the social media space as a whole—could be labeled *a* next big thing if not *the* next big thing, attracting an oversized share of marketers' attention and maybe even a portion of their advertising dollars. But I'd argue that we'd be looking at the forest when we should be studying the trees.

Big ideas, *big* campaigns, *big* buys, and of course "next *big* things" all held sway in the era of *big* media, when inventory was scarce, choice was limited, and consumer attention was seemingly abundant. But the tides have turned. Inventory and choice now approach the infinite, while attention has become the scarcest commodity of all. To paraphrase James Carse, the rules *must* change. I believe the new rules are grounded in a single, simple edict:

> *Think and act small*, because in the era of microcontent and microcultures the biggest marketing opportunities lie not in the one big thing but in lots and lots of small things.

And the small things can be very small indeed. Actually, they're not just small. They're micro: one blog post, a 60-second YouTube video, just one song (or maybe just the ringtone), a posted photo, a Facebook status update, a shared link, a single tweet. Any of these small things might sway the opinion of just one person. Any of them might drive thousands upon thousands of consumers into action.

This is what makes citizen uprisings like #iranelection not only possible today but more probable with each passing day, and lets a lone man dancing on a Pacific Northwest hillside entertain millions of people around the globe. And if marketers can harness the power inherent in these very same small things, we can achieve big results while spending less money on the spray-and-pray mass marketing efforts that have become less effective than ever before.

I call this new approach *micromarketing*, and I believe that companies—from the biggest of brands, to the scrappiest of start-ups, to individuals trying to make a difference—that tap directly into microcontent and microculture trends will not just survive but *thrive* in the post–mass marketing age.

Now, in order to join the micromarketing movement, you'll need to embrace seven shifts away from tried-but-no-longer-quite-so-true traditional approaches. These shifts are so important to the concept of micromarketing—and are so integral to the approaches, examples, case studies, and stories presented throughout this book—that I'd like to highlight them here.

THE SEVEN SHIFTS FROM MASS TO MICRO

	Mass Marketers...	microMARKETERS...
1	Rely upon *mass communications*	Resonate with *masses of communicators*
2	Broadcast messages over traditional *media networks*	Tap into the pass-along power and peer-to-peer potential of the *network effect*
3	Target consumers via *interruption*	Deliver mutual value through two-way *interactions*

	Mass Marketers...	microMARKETERS...
4	Plan campaigns around outdated concepts like the sales funnel, peak seasons and *prime time*	Make a commitment to engage people directly in *real time*
5	Buy *reach*	Build meaningful *relationships*
6	Aim for *awareness*	Earn *attention*
7	Hinge their success on *the one big thing*	Have their success through *lots and lots of small things*

In the chapters ahead, we'll consider each of the seven shifts in more detail while looking at concrete examples of how marketers of all shapes and sizes are applying micromarketing principles to achieve their goals and objectives, and finally we'll explore some of the ways *you* can do the right small things to get big results for your own company or clients. But first, let's dig deeper into what I mean when I say that *micromarketers think and act small.*

Thinking and Acting Small

Understanding the microMARKETING Mindset

"Getting bigger is not a marketing strategy.
Yet it's the only strategy many companies
seem to be using today. Line extensions,
mergers, acquisitions, multiple price
points and other techniques are obviously
designed to bulk up a company's sales.
But how do these techniques affect the
brand's position in consumers' minds?
In general, they weaken it."

—AL RIES, *ADVERTISING AGE*

"Great things are done by a series of small
things brought together."

—VINCENT VAN GOGH

SO SMALL, IT'S SCARY

I don't know many people who would say it's easy to make big money in the movie business these days. Truly great films are few and far between, production costs are through the roof, and a spate of bad reviews or unfavorable word of mouth can stop theatergoers in their tracks before even the first showing.

Still, most major studios release their fare into the crowded marketplace and try to fill seats by appealing to hordes of people with me-too marketing tactics, even across dramatically different genres. Whether the film is a slapstick comedy, weighty drama, action-packed thriller, or stately period piece, the 30-second spots are laden with quick cuts, one liners, context-free superlatives pulled from recent reviews, dramatic audio cues, and soundalike voice-overs. Each new release gets the usual run of full-page newspaper ads and a meticulously designed Flash Website that aims to draw online consumers into the story line even before they step foot into a theater. And more often than not, all of this is for naught; so many movies don't even earn enough at the box office to cover their own production costs.

State of Play, released by Universal Pictures in April 2009, is a perfect case in point. Based on the highly acclaimed British television serial of the same name, it was a big-budget, grown-up drama that told a complex, twisted tale about corrupt politicians running circles around nosy journalists. With a powerhouse cast featuring Academy Award winners Russell Crowe, Ben Affleck, and Helen Mirren, along with starlet Rachel McAdams, scores of favorable reviews, and a multimillion-dollar marketing push, the film had all the hallmarks of a Hollywood blockbuster. Despite all this, *State of Play* turned in a disappointing $10 million opening weekend and ended its run with a total box office haul of $39.4 million, some $20 million less than its $60 million production budget—a shortfall equal to Russell Crowe's leading-man salary.

Five months later, around the time *State of Play* was hitting people's Netflix queues, another film—this one written and directed by a first-time filmmaker, starring seven unknown actors, and shot nearly two years earlier, over the course of just seven days for a meager $11,558, with one video camera and at a single location—began a limited run in just 12 U.S. theaters. With its decidedly homegrown feel, this movie—a supernatural horror flick called *Paranormal Activity*—could hardly be more different from *State of Play* in just about every way, *including* its impressive results.

This little movie that could took in $77,873 during its low-key opening weekend, a gross that seems laughable compared with *State of Play*'s raw volume of nearly $40 million but one that delivered a stunning return on investment that earned out the film's budget nearly seven times over. Within a week of its late September 2009 release, at that point already showing in a total of 33 theaters in 20 markets, its total take reached $777,763, or

10 times its opening weekend gross; this was a virtually unheard of *70 times* return.

The following month, during the weekend of October 23, 2009—with the film's buzz on Twitter, Facebook, and other sites at a fever pitch—*Paranormal Activity* screened in nearly 2,000 theaters, topped the week's list of top box office draws, and earned another $21.1 million, bringing its five-week revenue figure to $61.5 million (nearly double *State of Play*'s total box office figure). The results shocked even Paramount Pictures, the major studio that had acquired the rights for the independently produced fright fest at Steven Spielberg's urging but approached its measured distribution with caution, a touch of skepticism, and virtually no mainstream marketing support. And though its run was only just beginning and the next few weeks would bring the expected print and television ad blitz, it's worth looking back at the path *Paranormal* followed to get to the $61.5 million milestone.

Almost a year earlier, a Santa Monica audience got its first introduction to Micah and Katie (the namesake lead characters portrayed by Micah Sloat and Katie Featherston) and a glimpse into their nightmare home populated by a malevolent spirit. Though *Paranormal Activity* had been shown at a few film festivals and cliquey gatherings of horror buffs—and had been previewed behind closed doors by a number of industry professionals, as its small-time producers sought a studio deal—this one show would mark its first screening for typical moviegoers and aim to prove that there might be a real market for the movie. Halfway through the show, people walked out, not because the film wasn't any good but because the gritty portrayal of the story's suspenseful, otherworldly (yet somehow believable) events were too frightening to bear. Among the watchers that remained, some literally screamed in fright as others clutched at one another for reassurance as minute after intense minute played out on the big screen. In a tableau that would become core to *Paranormal Activity*'s folklore, one girl sat alone in a corner of the theater, rocking back and forth with her face tucked between shaking knees.

According to *Paranormal*'s sales agent Stuart Ford, "We didn't plant that girl in the corner, I swear, she was just freaked out. As was everyone. It was pandemonium. Clearly, anyone who was in the room that night was left in no doubt that this movie works—it just has that effect."[1] In fact, the movie worked so well that Paramount signed on as distributor within 48 hours of that single screening. Even though Paramount knew it had a good movie on its hands, the company's executives were uncertain of exactly how large the market would be for the atmospheric, affecting yet undeniably amateur production, and they were at odds over what to do with the film. They decided to mitigate their risk and minimize their marketing expenditures until they knew more about the movie's odds for success.

Following a tentative test run of free late-night screenings in eight theaters, Paramount launched the film on September 25, 2009, with packed midnight shows in just 12 college towns, resulting in *Paranormal*'s stunning opening week performance. After seeing Twitter users flood the microblogging network with breathless 140-character endorsements like "Just got back from seein Paranormal Activity & I'm still LITERALLY shaking. Sleepin w/ the lights on tonight," and "I can't even spell right! Paranormal Activity is the scariest movie I've ever seen," Paramount approved a relatively modest and quite experimental marketing program that would put the film's fate directly in the hands of its potential audience and—if all went according to plan—would explicitly stimulate a significant amount of organic online word of mouth.

In a blog post published a few days after the initial 12-show screening, *Paranormal*'s first-time director Oren Peli invited readers to visit Eventful.com to *demand* that the movie play in their hometown multiplexes. This initiative marked the first time a major movie studio had partnered with Eventful[2]—a Web-based directory of real-world concerts, shows, nightclub appearances, sporting events, and other local happenings—and made use of its Demand It functionality[3] to engage consumers, generate grass-roots buy-in, and gauge the actual level of interest in a film. Peli's prompt—echoed in the Eventful call to action and picked up as a rallying cry by the horror and movie bloggers that wrote about the film and Paramount's unorthodox promotional activities—also encouraged demanders to Tweet Your Screams, thereby spreading word about the movie to their follower networks.

One tweet could have been lost in the stream. But hundreds of thousands of tweets from hundreds of thousands of different people, each with an individual tuned-in personal network, made a very real impact. Delivering upon its promise as "The First-Ever Major Film Release Decided by You," *Paranormal Activity* expanded into 33 theaters in the 20 most popular cities. Just one day later, Paramount announced that the movie would soon roll out to the 40 markets with the most votes, all chosen by theatergoers themselves.

Encouraged by the massive groundswell in organic social media support and the nearly instantaneous ROI of the movie's Demand It campaign, Paramount and Eventful soon issued an audacious challenge—the studio would give *Paranormal Activity* a full 1,000-plus screen run if fans made 1 million *demands*. "When [Paramount] saw the success of that early campaign, the big question mark at the studio level was does this thing deserve a nationwide release, and they were not sure," said Eventful president and chief executive Jordan Glazier. "So they put a big number out there and said, *hey, let the fans decide*."[4]

Glazier thought it would take the film a few weeks to reach the seemingly high benchmark. With the Tweet Your Screams call to action having the desired effect, the term *paranormal activity* and hashtag *#paranormalactivity* both firmly ensconced in Twitter's list of trending topics, a frenzy of YouTube activity as people flocked to the video site to watch the trailer, a rapidly growing community of fans on Facebook*, and spiking social media buzz, it actually took a mere four days for the movie's *demands* to top the seven-figure threshold.

In a detailed assessment of *Paranormal*'s marketing activities—a campaign that you might argue falls short in just about every area except its employment of a distinctly micro, social media–driven strategy—Movie Marketing Madness blogger Chris Thilk argues that other filmmakers could also achieve outsized results with similar approaches:

> With films that have niche appeal like this—whether it's a
> horror flick or a documentary about the plight of immigrant

---

* As I write this, the term Facebook uses to describe the relationships between consumers and brands is still evolving. As the social network is presently phasing out "become a fan" buttons and calls-to-action for the simpler "like" call-to-action, the people that choose to connect with a brand could ultimately be called almost anything—fans, followers, connections, subscribers, or even *likers*—by the time you read this book. Because today Facebook, its members, and the companies that maintain Pages on the network still use the term *fan*, I have chosen to stick with it throughout the text. I invite you to make a mental "global-replace" down the road.

farmers—an initial deployment to a targeted audience that's
then built on makes a lot of sense. Not all movies need to be
seen by everyone, but they do need to be seen by the audience that's likely to be interested in them.

That's why the "Demand It" idea is so intriguing and
something that I think could be widely adopted and adapted
by the independent film community. Come up with a list of
12 places to roll out the film at first and then let people literally demand the movie is brought to them based on that first
deployment. Get a critical mass in a location or two built up
and then make screening arrangements, arrangements that
are going to be easier to secure when a filmmaker who's
presenting the movie can say to a theater manager or whom-
ever that there are already 500 people who have committed
to come and see the film. Studio support is great, but this is
absolutely a tactic that can be utilized by anyone with an
internet connection and a movie to promote.[5]

Eschewing traditional and often ineffective movie marketing
approaches, Paramount didn't interrupt its way into people's living rooms, advertise its way to a massive opening weekend, or
hoodwink unsuspecting consumers into disseminating contrived
viral marketing messages. Rather, it empowered people to express
their interest, tell their friends and connections what they saw (to
"tweet their screams"), stake their personal claim (to *demand* the
film come to their local theaters), join a movement, and play a
direct role in *Paranormal*'s ultimate success.

And people did exactly those things. As Paul Dergarabedian,
box office analyst for Hollywood.com, put it, "On the social
networking sites, everybody's talking about how freaking scary

this movie is."[6] In an age when we've become accustomed to tuning out the hype manufactured by corporations and paid reviewers, it's amazing to see just how much impact hype can have when it comes directly from the mouths and keyboards of millions of real people just like us.

Today, there most likely isn't a soul at Paramount who's not a true believer in the very real business benefits of social media. "We all spend a lot of time talking about Facebook and Twitter and our ability to communicate," said Paramount's vice chairman Rob Moore. "Here's a case where it allows people to rally around a movie they care about and for them to have a sense of participation, then tell other people, *hey, this is something you should see too.*"[7]

Finally with Paramount's full support and backed with the studio's traditional marketing muscle, *Paranormal Activity* expanded to 160 theaters nationwide to satisfy some of the pent-up demand, as Paramount prepped for the rollout to screens nationwide. That weekend alone, the movie grossed $7.9 million at the box office and averaged a staggering $49,379 in revenue per theater—the highest ever per-screen average for a film playing in more than 100 venues.

One short week later it went on to its full nationwide release playing in nearly 2,000 theaters and, as of December 13, 2009, had earned more than $107 million during a 12-week run. It ranks as the fifth largest supernatural horror movie release of all time and the fourth highest grossing R-rated film of the year (edging out the much-hyped $130 million production, *Watchmen*, which hit theaters around the same time). Some argue that *Paranormal Activity* is the most profitable movie ever made, topping even the previous decade's most infamous virally marketed, lo-fi phenomenon, *The Blair Witch Project*. These would be impressive results for any major Hollywood release, but they're downright staggering for a gritty, low-budget independent that was scarcely able to find a major distributor.

microMARKETERS THINK AND ACT SMALL

The story of how *Paranormal Activity* achieved big results by doing a few small things right isn't simply a tale of movie marketing; it's a case study for micromarketing. And it would be a mistake to think that socially fueled, microdriven approaches like these are best suited to small brands, unlikely strivers, dark horses, distant underdogs, or niche players. Rather, in adopting a micromarketing mindset, it's not a matter of how big you are or how big you want to be. It's a matter of how small you behave in order to accomplish even the most audacious of goals. In fact, thinking and acting *anything but small* might do your company more harm than good. As Seth Godin wrote in *Small Is the New Big*:

> Big used to matter ... There was a good reason for this. Value was added in ways that suited big organizations. Value was added with efficient manufacturing, widespread distribution, and very large R&D staffs. Value came from hundreds of operators standing by and from nine-figure TV ad budgets. Value came from a huge sales force ... Recent changes in the way things are made and talked about mean that *big is no longer an advantage*. In fact, it's the opposite. If you want to be big, act small.

This is exactly why micromarketers go beyond traditional marketing's command-and-control, big-budget–big-box mentality and move in synch with microcontent and microculture trends. They understand that they can achieve big results by thinking and acting small, even if (*especially if*) they count themselves among the world's biggest brands—even if they're a global packaged goods powerhouse like Coca-Cola.

LIGHTNING IN A BOTTLE

In September 2008, Dusty Sorg and Michael Jedrzejewski—a couple of regular guys from Los Angeles—created a Facebook Page for their favorite soft drink, Coca-Cola. Theirs was just one of more than a hundred similar pages devoted to the beloved brand, but more so than the others, their tribute struck a nerve among fellow Coke lovers.

Facebook members searching for the soda's official presence (at the time, there was none) might have been attracted to the photograph Dusty and Michael chose as their Page's profile picture: a crisp, oversized beauty shot of Coke's iconic bottle that would be sure to stand out among the less arresting, low-resolution images associated with the other consumer-generated pages. Dusty and Michael might have simply had the right social graphs: people likely to join their friends' new page, motivated enough to participate, and connected enough to help the two founders spread the word to a larger network of interested consumers. Most likely though, it was nothing more than social media serendipity; perhaps it was simply the right page for the right product, at a time when most major brands were still just experimenting with their corporate Facebook strategies even though many consumers were already looking for ways to connect with and celebrate the lifestyle products they loved.

Visit Coke on Facebook

facebook.com/cocacola

As difficult as it is to attribute this particular Page's success to any single factor—or even to articulate a clear-cut winning formula—the results certainly could not be clearer. Within just a few months, the Page Dusty and Michael built had amassed more than a million fans, making Coca-Cola the biggest brand on Facebook even though the beverage giant's own marketing team had nothing to do with the effort. At a time when many marketers were scrambling to attract even a few thousand Facebook fans and struggling to keep those fans interested and engaged, two consumer evangelists had inadvertently cracked the code on behalf of their best bubbly beverage.

Coke had been dabbling with Facebook marketing for months—launching a series of applications and promotions that hadn't gained much traction among members of the popular social network—but had stopped short of creating its own Facebook Page. To Michael Donnelly, the Coca-Cola Company's group director of worldwide interactive marketing, the idea of creating your own fan club seemed rather inauthentic.

When I spoke with Donnelly, he explained, "For the most part, Fan Pages as we know them are really just *brand* pages. They're essentially Facebook destinations created by the companies themselves, rather than fan clubs started and operated *by* actual fans *for* actual fans." In his view, this approach amounts to little more than a misguided attempt to replicate a Web 1.0 approach in a Web 2.0 world. "When the Web first came along, companies built Websites and expected people to come to them. It's the same thing on Facebook. Companies are building their own Fan Pages and expecting people to come to them. But that's not what people do."

By contrast in the case of Coca-Cola, two real enthusiasts had created a proper fan club, and people *did* come. They came in droves and made it their own—starting discussions, sharing memories, uploading photos, and making new friends.

Needless to say, Coke's marketing leaders were monitoring its growth from a distance before eventually stepping in, not with a cease and desist, but with a helping hand. Donnelly is the first to admit Coke benefited from social serendipity: "This did fall in our laps, we'd be the first ones to say it. But what we do with it from now on is up to us." Today, Sorg and Jedrzejewski remain at the helm of their fan community while Coke lends its interactive marketing muscle both to grow the group's membership and to elevate the original pair from founders to "Facelebrities." In turn, the brand now has the ability to tap into a seven-figure opt-in network of enthusiasts for everything from participation to promotion. Today Coca-Cola's Page remains one of the most vibrant product-focused communities on Facebook, and the hub that grew out of the efforts of just two regular consumers is still dominated by the voice of the customer.

Everything Coke does in social media abides by a fan-first philosophy and aims to strike the right balance between truly organic consumer involvement and strategic brand participation. As

Donnelly puts it, "On Facebook, our fans create, upload, consume, and comment on their own user-generated, brand-related content. Coke listens, respects, and celebrates *their* manifestations of *their* brand while supplementing what the community itself is doing with our own content to support brand marketing objectives."

Industry watchers will recall that the Coca-Cola Company wasn't always so enthusiastic about celebrating other people's interpretations of its products and brands. When Fritz Grobe and Stephen Voltz—two other regular guys better known as EepyBird[8]—had a runaway viral video success with their 2006 clip of a sugary sweet fountain show created by dropping more than 500 Mentos mints into more than 100 bottles of Diet Coke, the candy maker was quick to capitalize on the attention by launching a contest that drew hundreds of copycat geyser makers. Coke, on the other hand, was quick to publicly chide EepyBird for the unorthodox use of its product. A company spokeswoman, Susan McDermott, told the *Wall Street Journal*, "We would hope people would want to drink [Diet Coke] more than try experiments with it," adding, "craziness with Mentos ... doesn't fit with the brand personality" of Diet Coke.[9] The Coca-Cola Company did eventually come around, partnering with EepyBird to field a brand-sanctioned geyser competition in October 2006 that proved to be a classic case of too little, too late.

It is perhaps somewhat ironic that I would feature a story about a corporate giant, a fixture of the Fortune 100, in a chapter about thinking and acting small, but the contrast between Coke in 2006 and Coke today provides a nice point of reference. At a time when many brands were trying—to generally lackluster effect—to manufacture viral video success stories in Madison Avenue conference rooms, Coke missed its best opportunity to cash in on a truly organic consumer-generated video phenomenon. Just a couple of years later, the company watched closely and then joined enthusiastically in a grassroots movement that began with just two consumers, but grew into a community of passionate fans. It became an authentic Facebook success story in the process.

THE SMALL (THINKERS) WILL INHERIT THE WORLD (WIDE WEB)

After many decades of thinking and acting big—decades during which biggest often implied best, even if the reality fell short of the promise—smart companies are finally discovering just how important it is to think and act small. The splintering of society into myriad microcultures and the microcontent explosion have made it necessary for marketers to retool their approaches to favor lots and lots of simple, small-scale activities over winner-take-all thinking, mass merchandise, big buys, and grand gestures.

In a micromarketing economy it is the little things that matter most, and it is the little things that can make a difference between merely surviving and outright thriving. *Twitterville* author Shel Israel did a great job of articulating the new world order in a 2009 blog post that touched upon the same shifts in culture, content, and commerce we're exploring in this book. He wrote:

> The entire world is becoming a micro market. We are self-organizing into topical niches. We decide about purchases in conversations that feel more like we are chatting over a

backyard fence than listening to voices that sound like they emanate from stadium public address systems.

We have entered into an era of micro marketing, of virtual one-on-ones. Platforms like Twitter allow each of us to have lots of such conversations when we wish to ... Social networks let single voices carry fast and far. We have entered into something new and different. Marketers need to understand the dynamic of hyperlocal micro markets and they have the tools to address them massively.

This is mass micro marketing and it turns market strategist minds upside down and inside out.[10]

The complete truth is that micromarketing doesn't only change our *thinking*. It changes our *actions*, turning how we go to market and the ways in which we relate to our customers upside down and inside out as well.

Paramount could have invested heavily to promote *Paranormal Activity* through traditional advertising. Instead it simply made it easy for moviegoers to sell the experience to one another, made consumers active partners and willing participants in the movie's success, and turned millions of raving fans into highly credible micromessage bearers. On Facebook, Coca-Cola didn't resort to costly giveaways, promotions, coupons, or gimmicks to build a massive presence. The company didn't need to mobilize people or recruit fans to participate, and it certainly didn't spend millions on advertising to direct Facebook members to a company-created presence on the network. The fans did the work for the company, self-organizing into a thriving seven-figure community that welcomed Coke's stepped-up participation when the brand partnered with the two real people who started it all.

In these two very different examples, we see the concept of micromarketing and the notion of *thinking and acting small* come to life in a number of ways. To name just a few:

➡ Eschewing tradition, learning new lessons while unlearning old ones, and being willing to zig where others might zag

➡ Treating individual customers as collaborators, colleagues, and coconspirators

➡ Realizing the potential of online peer-to-peer influence

➡ Recognizing the resonance of the voice of the consumer over the voice of the brand

➡ Tapping into the power of the few to reach the many

➡ Building brands and bottom lines fan by fan and 140 characters at a time

➡ Achieving impressive results over time by building on a series of small successes

In the stories told throughout this book, we'll see these same approaches (and many others like them) applied by a diverse group of global megabrands, fledgling microbrands, and everything in between. We'll begin by exploring how companies think and act small within the context of the first of seven shifts from mass to micro and, in the process, gain a clear understanding of the new dynamic that has emerged between marketers and their audiences as the media landscape has evolved from one dominated by a small handful of mass communicators to a large and growing mass of microcommunicators.

From Mass Communications to Masses of Communicators

Telling Your Brand Stories in the Voice of the Consumer

"For most of our lives, persuading people through technology channels like radio and TV belonged to the rich and powerful. That's changing quickly. Today, the potential to persuade is in the hands of millions. With these tools in hand, ordinary people sitting in dorm rooms and garages can compete against the biggest brands and the richest companies."
—Dr. B. J. Fogg

"We are small but we are many, we are many we are small; we were here before you rose, we will be here when you fall."
—Neil Gaiman, *Coraline*

THE AUDIENCE HAS AN AUDIENCE

The MTV Generation was defined by the content it consumed, the YouTube Generation by the content it creates. Emphasizing the change in behaviors over the change in media choices, marketing strategist Faris Yakob[1] has rechristened the latter the *Mediation Generation*, referring to the large and growing portion of the world's population that experiences life through the camera lens and has come to be defined "by the media it produces." By way of illustration, Faris advises, "Next time you are at a concert, look at all the people capturing the moment to mediate and broadcast it, to remember it and share it, to continue to create themselves with it."[2] The line between the stage and the stands has blurred, as the spectators have themselves become entertainers in their own rights.

Trendwatching.com, a leading consumer trends firm that draws its insights from a worldwide network of spotters, recognized this same shift as early as 2004 when it foretold the emergence of Generation C (which, like Faris's Mediation

Generation, isn't really a generation in the traditional sense of the word):

> No, this is not about a new niche generation of youngsters born between March 12, 1988, and April 24, 1993; the C stands for CONTENT, and anyone with even a tiny amount of creative talent can (and probably will) be part of this not-so-exclusive trend ... So what is it all about? The GENERATION C phenomenon captures the avalanche of consumer generated "content" that is building on the Web, adding tera-peta bytes of new text, images, audio and video on an ongoing basis ... The two main drivers fueling this trend? (1) The creative urges each consumer undeniably possesses. We're all artists, but until now we neither had the guts nor the means to go all out. (2) The manufacturers of content-creating tools, who relentlessly push us to unleash that creativity, using—of course—their ever cheaper, ever more powerful gadgets and gizmos. Instead of asking consumers to watch, to listen, to play, to passively consume, the race is on to get them to create, to produce, and to participate.[3]

In the intervening years, we have seen this new creative class emerge in earnest, staking their ground in a highly distributed microcontent environment that empowers everyone to be a media outlet and gives anyone the ability to be a not-so-hidden persuader. The members of this new and influential creative class might be *mediating* their own lives through content creation (in Faris Yakob's interpretation), but, just as important, they're *disintermediating* the centralized, advertising-supported channels of mass communications. On the social Web, consumer-generated content is not only created but also distributed without the intervention of gatekeepers or the ostensible benefit of old media infrastructure.

Indeed, some industry watchers estimate that as much as 62 percent of the content consumed by individuals born after 1980 comes not from professional programmers but from people they know personally. In other words, the people formerly known as the audience now have audiences of their own.

MEET THE MICROMAVENS

Steve Garfield is a lanky, fortyish Bostonian with a penchant for corduroy blazers, a passion for citizen journalism, and a knack for self-promotion that is rivaled only by his love of gadgets. Meet Steve in person, and you're likely to find yourself on the opposite end of his lens as he broadcasts real-time footage of your encounter to a few hundred or several thousand watchers on Qik, Ustream, or Livestream. He has been a content creator's content creator since 2004, when he became one of the Web's earliest video bloggers, one of a handful of social media pioneers who lifted their fingers from their computer keyboards, picked up digital cameras, and began delivering homegrown video content directly to consumers over the open airwaves of the World Wide Web.

Visit Steve Garfield's Video Blog

www.stevegarfield.com

During any given week, his output may include breaking coverage of a local news story, a practical step-by-step walk-through of a new piece of video equipment, a steady stream of mobile phone videos and photos shot during a live event, opinion pieces recorded in his Massachusetts home, or even raw footage documenting simple yet endearing slice-of-life moments from his personal life. Although he maintains his own network of personal blogs and social video channels, his best content has been picked up by popular podcasts like Rocketboom[4] or featured on mainstream media outlets such as Wired.com, the BBC, and CNN's consumer-powered iReport.[5] Because of his success, Steve's name is often on the short list when consumer electronics companies field promotions that put their latest gear directly in the hands of well-respected content creators and trusted online influencers.*

Steve Garfield is a micromedia mogul, a *micromaven*, a Web-savvy *new communicator* who understands that content is a valuable social currency and community is king. He is a one-man media outlet that draws an audience not through an exclusive relationship with a single, monolithic mass distribution partner, but through thousands upon thousands of relationships built directly with the individuals who follow his output across lots of small sites and who view his microchunked content on the larger networks that incorporate it into their own programming.

Steve is fueled by passion and powered by the tools of democratized content creation. And he is just one among many in an

---

* Disclosure: Powered has worked with Steve on behalf of Panasonic of North America.

era when the dominant mode of communications is shifting from mass to *the masses*. Just to name a few:

➥ Wine expert, entrepreneur, and author Gary Vaynerchuk has attracted millions of fans for his own video blog, Wine Library TV, and has tapped into a combination of Twitter, Tumblr, and one-on-one interaction to connect with consumers, demystify wine, grow his family's retail business, and establish himself as a personal branding tour de force.

> **Watch Wine Library TV**
>
> tv.winelibrary.com

➥ Through the LockerGnome technology blog network, the Geeks! online community, and his own 24-hour video lifecast, Seattle's Chris Pirillo provides a sizable army of enthusiasts with up-to-the-minute reviews and insider tips for the latest computers, electronics, gaming systems, and software.

> **Visit Chris Pirillo's Online Outposts**
>
> www.lockergnome.com
>
> geeks.pirillo.com
>
> chris.pirillo.com/live

➡ The helium-voiced Fred Figglehorn—a precocious, obnoxious (and mercifully fictional) six-year-old portrayed by Nebraska teen Lucas Cruikshank in three seasons' worth of self-produced Web videos, readymade for a predominantly tween and teen audience—boasts nearly 1.5 million YouTube channel subscribers, with the clips themselves routinely drawing seven-figure audiences.

> **Watch Fred's Videos on YouTube**
>
> www.youtube.com/user/fred

➡ Matt Halfhill is a sneaker fanatic who, through his NiceKicks blog, is among a small handful of influential mavens who tip the footwear trends that determine which designs will adorn the feet of millions of kids around the world.

> **Read the NiceKicks Blog**
>
> www.nicekicks.com

➡ Apparel marketing executives and members of fashion media's old guard alike are now taking their cues from photo bloggers like Jane Aldridge, the Texan high school student who publishes Sea of Shoes, and whose taste in high-end footwear and designer clothing has earned the attention of online fashionistas.

Visit Sea of Shoes

seaofshoes.typepad.com

The thing that differentiates micromavens from run-of-the-mill subject-matter experts is their mastery of the social Web; the thing that separates them from social media flukes—Internet flashes in the pan—is staying power. Most aren't exactly household names, but all are influential within their own microcultures, credible to their online communities, consistent in their creation of microcontent that appeals to their intended audiences. And as one-to-many mass marketing approaches falter, micromavens' influence, credibility, and proven ability to thrive in the microcontent age position them as a new class of many-to-many message bearers—prosumers capable of telling brand stories in a chorus of authentic, resonant, undeniably human voices.

THE POTENTIAL TO PERSUADE

In his 2000 book, *The Tipping Point*, Malcolm Gladwell wrote about "the law of the few," building upon the well-known 80-20 principle that stipulates that "in any situation roughly 80 percent of the 'work' will be done by 20 percent of the participants," but pointing out that "when it comes to [social] epidemics, though, this disproportionality becomes even more extreme: a tiny percentage of people do the majority of the work."

In Gladwell's view, "the success of any kind of social epidemic is heavily dependent on the involvement of people with a particular and rare set of social gifts." These influential few can be classified into three distinct categories, each playing its own unique role when driving widespread changes in beliefs and behaviors. *Mavens* are content creators, the knowledgeable experts who connect people to information about a given topic; *connectors* boast large personal networks populated with the right kinds of individuals and so are uniquely suited to connect people with one another; and *salesmen* wield the power of persuasion to convince individuals to band together into new groups and take action on new information.

Ten years later, thanks to the mainstreaming of the social Web, the democratization of technology, and the rise of Generation C, the mavens are no longer so few in number. But more important, the distinction between mavens and connectors has blurred if not disappeared altogether. People like Steve, Gary, Chris, Lucas, Matt, and Jane aren't just mavens; they're connectors too (and on a far larger scale than Gladwell might have considered when writing predominantly about analog world trends). And microcontent is their stock in trade, as they serve up information, entertainment, and ideas in containers that are small, convenient, and primed to travel from individual to individual— and group to group—throughout their large personal networks and beyond.

All of this begs an obvious question: if micromavens (as I've defined them) can be both mavens and connectors (by Gladwell's definitions), *can they be salesmen too?*

Some marketers are beginning to think so, as they find creative ways to engage the right audiences and get impressive results by employing one key micromarketing approach: eschewing big-budget media spends while giving masses of microcontent creators—or even just the right mavens—a compelling reason to share brand stories directly with online consumers.

THE PEOPLE'S PARTY

Until Ford Motor Company introduced its revamped lineup for the 2011 model year, the average American most likely hadn't seen a new Ford Fiesta driving down Main Street in her home town since people were cranking the Village People's new hit single "YMCA" on their very first Sony Walkmen, marveling at some of the earliest satellite photos taken of Jupiter's iconic rings, or contemplating how President Jimmy Carter might handle the hostage situation in Iran. Despite its popularity and longevity in Europe, the subcompact car had a remarkably short run in Ford's homeland right around the end of the 1970s before being dropped from the domestic lineup to make room for the newly introduced Escort.

Needless to say, you might assume that Ford would face some pretty hefty marketing challenges—from a general lack of awareness to a dearth of hipster credibility—if it were to reintroduce Fiesta as the "it" car for today's American 20-somethings. But in late 2009, the carmaker's marketing executives were contemplating ways to accomplish this unlikely feat in time for the subcompact's mid-2010 domestic relaunch. You might also expect that

Ford, one of the largest and most storied corporations in the world, might solve these challenges the same way it would have solved them in 1978—by leveraging its considerable spending power to field a shock-and-awe mass media advertising campaign. Yet this wasn't the road Ford traveled when it began marketing the vehicle a year before even the first 2011 model would be available on U.S. lots.

Instead, Ford loaned European-spec Fiestas to 100 young (and youngish) hyperconnected social media mavens for six full months as a means of earning attention, building evangelism, generating buzz, and sparking a movement (the *Fiesta Movement*, as Ford termed it) that offered the potential to deliver a return that far outstripped the company's relatively meager investment. In return for the opportunity to be among the first Americans to drive the new small car—the program launched in April 2009, well before the Fiesta's commercial availability—the 100 *agents* (as they were known) would participate in a series of themed challenges over the course of their six-month Ford affiliation.

The agents would compete in poetry slams and attend the Travel Channel Academy, take friends star sighting and scour their neighborhoods for celebrity look-alikes, challenge strangers to dance-offs and karaoke sing-offs, record original rap videos, and spoof popular films. They would use their content-creation skills to document their experiences in photos, videos, tweets, and blog posts, and their social networking savvy to distribute their micro-content across their own social media points of presence. Taking it one step further, the brand itself would aggregate the unfiltered feeds from all 100 micromavens on a Fiesta Movement conversation hub.

Visit the Fiesta Movement Hub
chapter1.fiestamovement.com

According to Ford's social media evangelist Scott Monty, "When you stop to consider that Ford Motor Company, a 106-year-old corporation, has loaned cars out for six months and is letting the agents say whatever they want, whenever they want, it's pretty groundbreaking. And aggregating all of that uncensored, unedited, raw content on one of our sites is even bolder."

Indeed, any program that puts not only the product but the message itself directly into the hands of its potential customers is a risky endeavor. The Fiesta Movement might have resulted in a flurry of negative reviews, product complaints, and Ford horror stories, all spotlighted on one of the brand's own Websites. Or perhaps worst of all, the agents might have stayed mum and produced little to no relevant content at all.

On the first count, Ford felt pretty confident that it had a quality vehicle and was bullish about its ability to prove it to the agents. In light of the Fiesta's 30-year run as a European top seller, the automaker was fairly certain it could make enthusiasts of a new generation of American buyers who hadn't driven (or even considered) a Ford lately.

Ford countered the second risk—the risk of a social marketing nonstarter—by choosing the right people to participate in the program. Among those Ford chose were top YouTube star

Judson Laipply,* lifecasting poster girl Jody Gnant,† and socially savvy visual artist Natasha Wescoat,[6] micromavens who had not only the inclination to tell stories and spread the word, but also the platforms and personal networks to garner attention and spark a groundswell in peer-to-peer conversations about the Fiesta.

But even more important than tapping the right communicators, Ford stacked the cards for success by choosing the right nontraditional approach, one that was well aligned with the essence of the car itself. As Scott puts it:

> The Fiesta Movement is a program that is custom built for this car. The Fiesta is our first global platform car, our top-selling vehicle in Europe, launched in China in January 2009, but won't be built in North America until the second quarter of 2010. With the Fiesta Movement kickoff in April 2009, we'll have had over a year's worth of buzz generated about the vehicle, entirely through nontraditional media, by the time the new model is for sale here in the States. And the digital influencers we've chosen—the "socially vibrant," as we call them—are largely from the very demographic that we hope will buy the new Fiesta. They eat, sleep, and breathe the Internet, and they're thrilled to have the opportunity to be one of just 100 people who have this car that isn't available to anyone else in the country yet. So naturally, they tell everyone about it. With a program like Fiesta Movement,

---

* Laipply's "Evolution of Dance" has ranked as YouTube's most-watched video for more than three years: bit.ly/laipplydance.
† Gnant's photo literally appears within Wikipedia's definition of *lifecasting*: bit.ly/wikipediagnant.

Ford gets kudos as a company that "gets it," as a company that is even hip and cool. Considering that the Fiesta is a car that exudes cool—yes, people are increasingly thinking of our designs as *cool*—the marketing is completely consistent with the product itself.

All of this sounds great in theory, a textbook case of social marketing done right. But the proof is in the performance. If Ford had set out simply to shift perceptions among a small set of protoconsumers, providing the agents with good cars and great experiences would have been enough. But ultimately, Ford was banking on the ability of its handpicked network of 100 message bearers to harness the Web's network effect and influence a much larger audience of potential buyers.

Ford has estimated that the agents' Fiesta Movement–related content, which was created and distributed over the course of the six-month program, delivered more than 10 million earned media impressions, all *without a single dollar* of paid media spend and an *overall* investment far lower than it would have made to field a more traditional mass marketing campaign. According to data released by Ford Motor Company, that number comprises:

- 6 million YouTube video views

- More than 3.7 million estimated Twitter impressions

- 740,000 Flickr photo views

Ford attests that the resulting brand-name recognition for the not-yet-available Fiesta had reached 60 percent by the end of the Fiesta Movement, a notable level of awareness rivaling that of equivalent models marketed and sold in North America for two to three years. And this is exactly the type of awareness Ford needed to resonate with a Generation Y audience that would rather learn about a new product from 100 "people just like me" than from the centenarian manufacturer's official spokesperson. As a final measure of success, through this program Ford accumulated a database of more than 80,000 hand raisers who expressed interest in learning more about the 2011 model as soon as vehicles arrived in dealer showrooms—97 percent of these people didn't drive Ford vehicles at the time.

ISLANDS IN THE STREAM

If marketing a relatively unknown new model of car to a notoriously hard-to-engage audience more than a year before its general availability seems like a difficult job, marketing an island paradise would appear to be an easy one. Beautiful beaches, incredible weather, friendly locals, and breathtaking scenery: the market would likely be vast and the appetite for dream vacations virtually unlimited. Perhaps Hamilton Island, one such paradise nestled up alongside Australia's Great Barrier Reef, is the exception to the rule—or maybe it's just a reminder that in this world not everything is as it seems.

Embroiled in debt throughout the 1990s, Hamilton Island was sent into receivership—a form of bankruptcy—long before the global economic downturn in 2008 would choke consumer spending and dash many people's hopes of daydream-inducing holidays on island paradises. In 2003, Australian billionaire Robert Oatley purchased the ersatz paradise for approximately

$200 million. But the task of revitalizing a tropical wonderland would prove more difficult than most would imagine, and as Oatley engineered his island's turnaround, the looming recession only served to exacerbate the situation. Cash-strapped travelers weren't exactly lining up at ticket counters to book their trips to Queensland, the Australian territory that counts the natural beauty of the Great Barrier Reef and the sea-sun-and-sand life-style of Hamilton Island among its chief tourist attractions. And so Tourism Queensland, facing its own budget restrictions and recession-era belt tightening, learned that filling Hamilton Island hotel rooms and putting bodies on beaches is not as simple as a holiday in the sun.

Armed with a mere $1.2 million in funding—roughly the amount of money it takes to run just one 30-second spot just one time during the season finale of *American Idol* and reach less than 9 percent of the population of the United States alone—Tourism Queensland posed its agency, SapientNitro, a thorny challenge: despite a budget that many big-brand marketers would brush off, build enough worldwide awareness to drive a meaningful turn-around in bookings. Fortunately, the solution was rather simple. Think small, act small, and offer one micromaven a job.

In early 2009, classified ads cropped up in the backs of news-papers around the world, and job postings appeared on employ-ment Websites like Monster.com. Tucked among thousands of unassuming ads for uninspiring accounting, administrative, and advertising positions, these ads promised the right candidate "The Best Job in the World" and pointed interested applicants to the Website IslandReefJob.com.

Rooted in the reality that *staying and playing* beats *telling and selling*, SapientNitro sidestepped the industry-standard mass media mix of travel site banner buys, television spots, and full pages in Sunday newspaper travel sections (it couldn't have afforded much anyway) to launch a micromarketing campaign grounded in a big idea. If you don't truly experience something until you've immersed yourself in it, then the right person could experience more of the Barrier Reef by living on it.

Best Job was a global competition, inviting any individuals with passion, creativity, personality, and a camera to record a 60-second video explaining to Tourism Queensland, as well as to their personal networks and (more important) the world, why they were the perfect candidate for what Tourism Queensland called "a prize that isn't a prize, it's a job." That job, for all intents and purposes, was a six-month paid vacation on Hamilton Island, where the winner would live rent-free in a three-room villa and earn a hefty AUD$150,000 salary for experiencing the best the barrier reef has to offer and documenting it all in blog posts, photos, and videos posted to IslandReefJob.com.

Read the Island Caretaker Blog

islandreefjob.com

Far from a mere job search, the Best Job in the World was a prime example of how brands can achieve outsized results by putting both the message itself and the distribution of the message into the hands of a good-sized army of microcontent creators. While finding the one right person for the position—someone capable of holding the interest of world travelers for the entire six-month stint, a micromaven they could call their own—was clearly important to the success of the program, the real goal was "to tell the rest of the world we really are open for business," according to Tourism Queensland's CEO, Anthony Hayes. And for the most part, Queensland would deliver this message in the voice of the consumer, with no additional paid media advertising beyond the original classified postings.

While Tourism Queensland couldn't have purchased enough interruption advertising to build mass awareness, it hoped it could achieve its goals by appealing directly to consumers themselves and inspiring them to create and post a massive amount of brand-relevant consumer-generated content. Ford's Fiesta Movement built traction through the efforts of just 100 carefully chosen agents. The Best Job in the World aimed to build a veritable tidal wave of awareness by recognizing that—in the age of microcontent—anybody can be a creator, everyone is a connector, and (harnessed properly) thousands of people would do a pretty good job of selling the idea of Queensland getaways to themselves, one another, and the population at large.

In terms of numbers, Tourism Queensland expected to attract 400,000 Website visitors over the course of the entire competition, resulting in 14,000 consumer-generated videos promoting the islands, and then engage the larger online population in a massive community voting process resulting in a short list of front-runner candidates. When IslandReefJob.com logged more than 200,000 visits on just the first day of the campaign, it was already obvious that by thinking small Queensland and SapientNitro had happened upon something quite big. Soon the social media sphere was buzzing with chatter about the program—as well as talk of Hamilton Island, the Great Barrier

Reef, and Queensland—as a direct result of the applicants' own blog posts, tweets, social networking activities, and grassroots promotional efforts geared toward increasing their odds of making the final cut.

By the time Tourism Queensland awarded the Best Job in the World to an Englishman named Ben Southall, the program had amassed 34,684 applicants from 197 countries who created and posted 610 hours' worth of 1-minute video clips—enough original content to make approximately 332 feature films and a far cry from the mere 30 seconds of U.S. television airtime Tourism Queensland might have purchased with its $1.2 million budget. As Tourism Queensland narrowed the pool to 50 contenders and then homed in on its top 10 picks, more than 475,000 people cast votes to select 1 lucky fan favorite as the "wild card" 11th finalist.* Ultimately, IslandReefJob.com drew more than 6.8 million monthly unique visitors who spent an average of 8.25 minutes on the site.

As staggering as those results may be, they pale in comparison to the media impressions Tourism Queensland earned despite the fact that it couldn't afford to buy them. As we saw in the cases of #iranelection, the Sasquatch Dancing Man, and pretty much every other example I've shared so far, when something interesting bubbles up through the masses, traditional mass communications outlets often take notice. More than 22 international news crews flew to Hamilton Island to report on the arrival of the finalists, producing 86 broadcast interviews in just 3 days. Winner Ben Southall personally conducted an

---

* In the end, a total of 16 finalists, including fan favorites, were invited to Queensland for in-person interviews.

additional 100 print, TV, and radio interviews within the first 24 hours of his stint as Island Caretaker (the actual title associated with the Best Job).

SapientNitro has estimated that the program reached an audience of 5 billion through as much as AUD$207 million in unpaid media coverage—everything from CNN, Fox, and Sky News stories, Travel Channel appearances, a *Today Show* nod as one of the world's coolest positions, *Time* and *National Geographic* magazine articles, and a BBC documentary to YouTube viewership of the audition videos themselves and 231,355 blog mentions.[7] While the mainstream television and print coverage is notable and the sheer volume of blogosphere coverage is significant, the value of the candidate-created videos and the grassroots support from the YouTube community that housed many of those videos should not be underestimated.

In fact, Australian marketing blogger Tim Burrowes[8] credited social media and organic word of mouth with driving the program's runaway success.

> This is probably the first time that a campaign has achieved this sort of reach with so little advertising spend other than a few strategically placed job ads ... This has all been about the power of the people passing things on, largely through YouTube. The main lesson to be learned here is that if you have an original, exciting idea that gets people talking, you don't need to spend huge on advertising.[9]

Of course, talk is worse than cheap if it doesn't deliver tangible business results—and Tourism Queensland's Hayes didn't mince words when he told reporters, "The key now ... is to convert the global interest raised by the Best Job in the World into visitors to Queensland—to bring more tourist dollars into Queensland's economy, protect existing tourism jobs and hopefully create new ones."[10]

Judging by the resulting 82 percent increase in bookings to the island resort, JetBlue's scramble to open a new direct route between Sydney and Hamilton Island, and (according to Tourism Queensland's own *Annual Northern Summer 2009 Report*) a 44 percent year-over-year increase in weekly seat capacity for flights between the United States and Queensland, the Best Job in the World proved its ability to increase more than just awareness and conversation. It increased consideration and demand. And that should have not only satisfied Hayes, but put Robert Oatley on the road toward recouping his $200 million investment in Hamilton Island.

WHAT'S YOUR DISINTERMEDIATION PLAN?

Ford had one when it eschewed mass media advertising and introduced a cool new car to Gen Y buyers by tapping into the talents of 100 hand-chosen micromavens. Queensland Tourism had one when it parlayed a classified advertising budget into a massive groundswell of attention and action that even money couldn't have bought. To make the most of the shift from mass communications to masses of communicators, you should have one too.

Any marketer can apply lessons from the Fiesta Movement and the Best Job in the World—and learn from the micromavens themselves—to turn disintermediation into new strategies for attracting attention and directly connecting with the right audiences. Let's consider just three approaches that can deliver results for virtually any business.

Turn Micromavens into Enthusiasts

Done right, programs like the Fiesta Movement work because they create a win-win scenario for both brand and advocate. They offer a chance to experience a new product in a deep and meaningful way, serve to bring the brand's promise to life, prove that this promise is matched with a consistent reality, and provide the participants with clear and compelling reasons to spread the word. I often talk to marketers about the importance of giving influencers both a reason to *believe* (to buy into the value proposition, to become a true fan) and a reason to *behave* (to take action and encourage their communities to do the same). Talk to lifecaster Jody Gnant about her experiences as a Fiesta Movement agent, and it becomes clear that Ford's program hit the mark:

> The Fiesta Movement changed the way I think about Ford. They gave 100 cars to 100 people with pretty good social media reach and said, "Say what you will about the car—just be honest." That really speaks to the quality of the vehicles they're putting out there. And I had absolutely zero complaints about my Fiesta. It wasn't just the nicest economy car I've ever driven; it even compares well to the *more expensive cars I've driven!*
>
> But the Ford Fiesta Movement also changed my life. When Ford gave me the car, I really needed it. My own

vehicle had been out of service for about 12 months. Plus they gave me the most unbelievable summer I've ever had. They taught me to take chances, push boundaries, and grow with each monthly mission. They treated me like I was part of the Ford family, and I believe that we *are* a family with all my heart. I will always look to Ford when it comes time to buy a car, because Ford was there for me when I needed them most—and because I know that people like Scott Monty and [Fiesta's brand manager] Sam De La Garza will actually hear my needs.

Companies can all learn a lot of lessons from what Ford has done: the way they reinvented themselves while staying true to their brand, proving that a big company can care, their stellar entrance into the social media space, and last but not least, their focus on being the best American car-maker . . . period. I will always love Ford, because Ford loved me first.

Inspire, Celebrate, and Elevate Microcontent Creators

Today's best micromaven-oriented marketing programs improve upon early consumer-generated advertising competitions by emphasizing "what's in it *about* me" over "what's in it *for* me." While free Fiestas and a chance to land the opportunity of a life-time provided plenty of tangible incentive to the content creators that participated in the Ford and Tourism Queensland programs, both delivered outsized results by inspiring Generation C micro-mavens to *continue creating themselves* through brand-relevant content. This micromarketing approach is becoming more and more common among big brands.

Before Ford selected its U.S. agents, the automaker embarked on a yearlong pan-European collaborative photography project that invited anyone with a camera and a point of view to share his or her personal interpretations of "now" (in synch with the Fiesta's European tagline, "This Is Now") in a brand-sponsored Flickr group. The group, which has attracted more than 6,000 members who have submitted over 7,000 visually arresting images—the best of which were showcased throughout the year on Ford Europe's This Is Now blog despite the fact that almost none featured Ford, the Fiesta, or even automotive motifs—is now entirely consumer-run and remains active even after the sponsored project has come to an end.

See the This Is Now Photographs

www.flickr.com/groups/thisisnow

www.thisisnow.eu

Meanwhile back in the colonies, Levi's—an American apparel icon with nearly as much history as the nation itself—initiated a similar open call, asking the "Yes We Can" generation to define and document what it means to be American in 2009. The social marketing elements of its "Go Forth" advertising inspired a mass of Millennials to bridge the past, present, and future by rewriting the Constitution and creating a collaborative portrait of everyday American life. The latter resulted in an evocative panorama of first-person microcontent storytelling, a digital patchwork made entirely of thousands of citizen-generated photos, videos, audio recordings, and text messages.

Make the Leap from Mass Communicator to Microcurator

As Edelman SVP and top digital trends blogger Steve Rubel has written on his personal lifestream, "Information sources are exploding ... Attention is finite. We're becoming media agnostic, but when we're interested in something we dig down into our interests."[11] As consumers face ever-rising demands on their attention in the infinite channel present, marketers can reestablish relevancy, create valuable microcontent assets, and forge direct conduits to prospects and customers by superserving those interests. Aggregating and curating—even adding some much-needed context to—the sometimes daunting flow of existing Generation C content lets marketers tap into the microcontent phenomenon without necessarily placing bets on specific mavens. If every person is a media producer, curation allows any company to launch its own direct-to-consumer media network.

IBM leverages its heritage as an information technology leader while tapping into a Web-wide conversation about sustainability with a long-running microblog that supports the company's A Smarter Planet marketing push. This stand-alone site, built on the popular and decidedly consumer-grade Tumblr platform, aggregates snippets of topical and noteworthy text, images, and videos from across (to quote A Smarter Planet itself) "a Web Wide World that is instrumented, interconnected and intelligent." Similarly, the UPS-"delivered" popurls Brown Edition offers businesspeople a near-real-time dashboard of trending business stories harvested from across the blogosphere, microchunked from mainstream media, and produced specifically for UPS by recognized business and technology micromavens.

See the Content IBM and UPS Curate

smarterplanet.tumblr.com

brown.popurls.com

Through a Twitter mash-up—a stand-alone Web page that uses data from the public tweetstream to provide a new service that presents the data in an original way—called OPEN Forum Pulse, American Express helps small-business owners find value and relevance on the infamously noisy microblogging service. Rather than impart American Express's own advice or present the opinions of a cherry-picked roster of well-known business experts (things Amex does well through other portions of a larger OPEN Forum community experience), Pulse simply curates the Twittersphere's most salient conversations by, for, about, and among small businesses; delivers them in real time; and allows site visitors to further filter this still massive pool of microcontent by industry and company name. This is both a classic instance of a big brand delivering marketing as a service and an innovative way to tap into the collective wisdom of the most micro of mavens.

Visit OPEN Forum Pulse

pulse.openforum.com

PSSSST ... PASS IT ALONG

While traditional marketers achieve scale in direct proportion to the money they spend to reach the masses, hitting critical mass with micromarketing can be a more complex proposition. Even the best microcontent initiatives, undertaken in partnership with the right micromavens, are bound to underwhelm if nobody feels compelled to spread the word. One of the themes running through the stories I've shared is that success lies at the point where creation meets connections, where content meets community.

In the next chapter, we'll explore what viral *really* means.

From Media Networks to the Network Effect

Engaging Audiences in the Age of Human-Powered Distribution

"In nature we never see anything isolated,
but everything in connection with
something else which is before it,
beside it, under it and over it."
—JOHANN WOLFGANG VON GOETHE

"I told two friends and they told
two friends. And so on and so on
and so on ..."
—FABERGE ORGANICS SHAMPOO
COMMERCIAL (1980S)

WE'RE ALL IN THIS TOGETHER

It's September 2, 2009. A man clothed in a heather gray hoodie, his identity obscured entirely by a plastic mask depicting a grinning, mustachioed Guy Fawkes, stands before a blank wall. Wordlessly, as the plaintive instrumental strains of "First Breath after Coma" by a band called Explosions in the Sky provide the only audio cues, the man extends his open hand toward the camera's lens. He has written three words across his palm in thick, black ink: "Say It Clearer."

It is a call to action that sends ripples of excitement through the YouTube community, not so much for what it is but for what it represents. Nearly three years after inspiring what ABC News called "a tidal wave of connection," MadV is trying to do it again.

See MadV on YouTube
bit.ly/see-madv

Back in April 2006, an anonymous (and enigmatic, as it would turn out) YouTube member, known only by the handle *MadV*, began uploading half-minute clips of himself performing magic tricks. Each bore the video artist's signature style: MadV's face was always concealed by a replica Guy Fawkes mask similar to the one popularized in Alan Moore's *V for Vendetta* graphic novel; his performances were devoid of any spoken words but were often accompanied by evocative music. His creativity and his skills as a magician attracted as many as 2 million viewers, caught the attention of the YouTube team who featured his best-known illusion on the site's home page, and spawned hundreds of imitators. Over the course of just four weeks, he entertained YouTube's early adopters with nine flawlessly performed minor miracles—object levitations, antigravity tricks, disappearances, and manifestations—before performing a different kind of vanishing act: bidding his newfound fans goodbye and leaving the site for an alleged television production deal that never seemed to materialize.

But six months later, MadV was back on YouTube with another half-minute video in which he presented not an illusion, but an invitation. The clip showed the man in his familiar costume, first writing on his hand and then holding his palm toward the camera. And on that palm appeared the handwritten words, "One World." The text accompanying the upload, though still somewhat cryptic, elaborated on MadV's request that anyone seeing the video follow his lead:

> This is an invitation, to make a stand, to make a statement, to make a difference. Join in. Be part of something. Post your response now. 4/12/06 *

---

* December 4, 2009, written in the European standard format.

Visitors logging on to YouTube once again found Guy Fawkes's grinning visage featured on the home page, and word began to spread among the video sharing site's rapidly growing user population. "One World," as the video was titled, became YouTube's "Most Responded Video of All Time," as more than 2,000 people around the world promptly responded to MadV's call to arms in the days following its upload—recording and posting Webcam clips of themselves writing their own words on their own hands before silently extending their open palms toward the lens.

Just before Christmas 2006, MadV posted "The Message," a four-minute sequence threading together dozens of responses to his "One World" invitation. It is a voiceless, but unmistakably emotional, montage of YouTube users of a variety of ages, genders, and nationalities all delivering personal messages of love, promise, unity, and hope, appeals for change, words of encouragement to the world's lonely and disenfranchised. Through MadV's edit, Generation C told watchers around the world "we are all connected," "love yourself," "I believe in you," "think," "tread gently," "open your eyes," "don't quit!" and, enigmatically, "they could be gone tomorrow!" And then MadV was himself gone from YouTube once again, taking much of his microcontent down in the process, posting new content infrequently over the following three years.

Watch "The Message" on YouTube
bit.ly/madv-themessage

The September 2 upload in which MadV urged viewers to "Say It Clearer," a clip titled "One World—HD," marked his return; and the reason for his return became quite clear to anyone who saw the new video: repeat the success of "One World" and "The Message" but upgrade the finished product to take advantage of YouTube's higher-quality high-definition format. This time around, more than 265,000 viewed the calling, and 464 responded, leading to MadV's next community crowdsourced creation. On November 5, 2009—Guy Fawkes Night in the United Kingdom—he presented a "Message"-like mash-up of the best responses dubbed "We're All in This Together." Although it didn't quite measure up to the original, the result is equally affecting and remains a valid illustration of just one of the ways in which the social Web forges new, previously unseen, technically impossible connections among people.

Watch "We're All in This Together"

bit.ly/inthistogether

CANCER IS A VIRUS

Just a few days before "We're All in This Together" clocked its first YouTube view, Drew Olanoff walked out of his doctor's office cancer-free. Over the course of the previous five months, ever since he had announced his illness in a blog post, more than 14,000 friends and strangers (mostly strangers) blamed everything—from late flights and faulty hard drives to bad hair days and cold coffee—on Drew's cancer. While this might sound insensitive at first blush, it was just what the doctor ordered. The power of all these people taking cancer to task had helped Drew beat the dreaded disease into submission.

Read Drew Olanoff's Blog Post
bit.ly/drewolanoff

Drew Olanoff is a long-time citizen of the social Web who knows a thing or two about fostering community. Since 1996 he has earned his living by managing projects and leading communities for a variety of Web start-ups, while honing his microcontent chops through his *Best Damn Tech Show* podcast and *scriggity* Web video show. A serial early adopter with considerable micro-maven credibility, Drew was often the first kid on his block to try new social services. Long before the average person had even heard of Twitter, Drew was already tweeting up a storm as @drew (yes, just @drew—no last name, last initial, qualifier, or signifier). His passion for technology is matched by his commitment to people, a commitment he has demonstrated with efforts like Gmail4Troops—a program he cofounded in 1994 to put 10,000 then-scarce invites for Google's high-capacity e-mail service into the hands of U.S. troops looking for a better way to share memories with their loved ones at home.

When Drew landed a dream job as director of community at Los Angeles–based mobile media company GOGII, everything seemed to be going his way. And then Drew noticed a lump in his neck and, on May 20, 2009, was diagnosed with stage III Hodgkin's lymphoma.

In a move that was a bit irreverent but right on brand for the pierced and tattooed 29-year-old, and more than a bit community-minded, Drew urged Twitter members—an online population already inclined toward airing grievances in public—to #blamedrewscancer whenever something didn't quite go as planned. Not only would Drew find personal solace in the outpouring of support; he also reasoned that #blamedrewscancer might be a good mechanism for raising cancer awareness and spurring an upswing in charitable donations to support cancer-related charities. His reasoning was sound—among other cause-oriented initiatives, the Twitter community banded together in 2007 to create and support the Frozen Pea Fund,[1] a grassroots fund-raising organization that generated thousands in donations for cancer research in honor of breast cancer patient Susan Reynolds, a fixture of Twitter's early adopter community.

Visit Blame Drew's Cancer

www.blamedrewscancer.com

Word of Drew's cancer—and the #blamedrewscancer campaign—began to spread virally among the Twitterati, starting with Drew's own circle of friends but soon spilling beyond his personal network into a larger community of connected strangers around the world. As the number of #blamedrewscancer tweets rapidly rose into the thousands, Drew assumed he could garner the support of corporate sponsors that might like the idea of coupling social media with cause marketing, of tapping into the brand-building potential of the rapidly growing Twitter network while contributing to the greater good. Instead—absent any corporate involvement—Drew's efforts remained grassroots, driving more than $10,000 in donations to various cancer-related charities from individuals over the course of the summer, even without the support of a big brand backer.

While much of the support—both emotional and financial—grew organically, Drew spurred interest and participation with a series of well-timed gimmicks. First, he raised $2,112 for the Make-A-Wish Foundation by offering to tattoo the highest bidder's Twitter handle on his arm. Then, recognizing that his *own* Twitter handle—simply @drew—was a more valuable asset than a strip of unmarked skin, he announced on October 3, 2009, that he would auction that to the highest bidder, in support of Lance Armstrong's LiveStrong. And then something really interesting happened.

Actor and *The Price Is Right* host Drew Carey—relatively new to Twitter and saddled with the cumbersome handle @DrewFromTV—caught wind of the auction and tweeted a $25,000 bid, then quadrupled his offer to $100,000 provided his own follower count reached 100,000 by Olanoff's birthday on November 9. Drew Carey's involvement resulted in a flurry of mainstream media coverage and sparked more momentum for the cause, driving Carey to raise the stakes again, pledging $1 million if he reached 1 million followers by year-end (or a pro rata amount calculated at $1 per actual follower if he didn't hit that seven-figure milestone). Near the end of 2009, Carey's follower count was approaching 300,000 with a goal to donate $294,433 with a couple of weeks left before the New Year's Eve deadline. But as the year drew to a close and the deadline approached, Carey once again changed the rules to keep the ultimate seven-figure goal within his sights: he announced that he would indeed donate the full $1 million when the combined follower count for @drewfromtv and @livestrong hit the 1 million mark, no matter when it happens.

In the meantime, Drew Olanoff has relinquished his coveted @drew moniker, reserving it for Carey's use—Olanoff now tweets as @thatdrew—and continues to innovate with new social charity models through his own nonprofit foundation known simply as Blame Cancer.[2]

Follow Drew and Drew on Twitter
www.twitter.com/thatdrew
www.twitter.com/drewfromtv
www.twitter.com/drew

In a hyperconnected society where *we're all in this together*, one man's personal ordeal started and sustained a movement fueled by little more than his own determination to be a survivor, the grassroots support of his community, and the social Web's unprecedented ability to support the peer-to-peer spread of information. The #blamedrewscancer movement has amassed a supportive crowd tens of thousands strong and has already resulted in hundreds of thousands of dollars in cancer charity donations. It will benefit cancer sufferers who have never even heard the name *Drew Olanoff*, and its effects will long outlast Drew's own battle against the disease. Though nothing could have been further from Drew's mind, #blamedrewscancer—like MadV's story before it—also holds some valuable lessons for marketers looking to accelerate the spread of messages in an age during which traditional one-to-many broadcast networks are giving way to many-to-many human networks.

FEED ME, STREAM ME, LIKE ME, LINK ME

Throughout our lifetimes, and for many lifetimes before ours, our experiences of the day's events have been defined by, documented through, even dominated by broadcast media. We've grown up in a mass age during which our entertainment experiences and access to information came to us largely over television and radio airwaves of course, but also in newspapers, between the covers of magazines, plastered across roadside billboards, in our curbside and electronic mailboxes, and even displayed alongside the content offered by Web 1.0 mass-reach stalwarts AOL, MSN, and Yahoo! All these forms of media thrived in an era when content, choice, and the means of distribution were relatively scarce but consumers' capacity for attention was seemingly abundant.

The general business model should be a familiar one: the few created or commissioned one-size-fits-many programming that appealed to the broadest possible swathe of the population, and then replicated it across controlled, linear, predominantly one-way channels designed for the express purpose of delivering just this type of content to the masses. If you were a mass marketer, you aped the predominant media model in an effort to fit seamlessly into the content flow. You too created content—in the form of advertising messages—to appeal to a similarly broad population, then replicated it over and over by paying (or in the case of public relations, pitching) to have it inserted into a lineup of ostensibly appealing programming. That was then; this is now.

In Chapter 3 we explored this same theme by looking at the shift from mass communications to masses of communicators, the emergence of Generation C and the rise of micromavens, and social media's role in empowering the entertained and informed to themselves evolve into entertainers and informers. But there is perhaps a more powerful, more pervasive shift to consider: in the microcontent age, at the dawn of a postmedia era in which controlled channels and destination media are giving way to the not-so-controlled chaos of the social Web, everybody—regardless of the extent to which a person creates his or her own original content—is a *programmer*.

Joe Marchese is the cofounder of SocialVibe,[3] a marketing solutions provider that rewards social network members for sharing branded assets with their personal circles of friends, fans, and followers by making microcontributions to charitable causes. Because person-to-person dissemination of content is central to his business model and critical for his clients' success, he spends a lot of time thinking about why, how, when, and where microcontent gets distributed among peer networks on the social Web. And one of the springboards for his thinking is the fact that so much of the microcontent we're exposed to on the social Web comes to us chosen, filtered, curated, and contextualized by the people we count among our friends and online connections—regardless of who produced it and where it might actually reside. As Joe puts it:

> You can think of the world of social media as a world of millions of people programming content for friends, co-workers, and total strangers, starting conversations and directing traffic. So if I follow 200 people on Twitter or have 200 friends on Facebook, I'm really subscribing to 200 small-scale niche content programmers. The content they choose to share—pictures, videos, links to other Websites—comes to me as feeds. Feeds like Twitter status updates and the Facebook news feed.

When Joe speaks of feeds, he is hitting upon an important social Web concept: content streams or social activity streams. Streams—always-on feeds of microcontent, status notifications, links, recommendations, and more, posted by our online friends and connections, pushed into a time-ordered flow of bite-sized updates presented on our social networking presences and in mobile applications—have become a (if not *the*) central feature of consumers' social media experience. Some people, like prominent blogger Jeff Jarvis, have argued that streams represent the next phase of not only social media but the media industry as a whole. In a November 2009 blog post, Jarvis wrote, "Media can't expect us to go to it all the time. Media has to come to us ... Content will insinuate itself into streams and streams will insinuate themselves back into content. The great Mandala."[4]

While streams might figure prominently in the social media present and represent one possible vision for mainstream media's future, the idea itself is rooted in the decade-old concept of lifestreaming—a decidedly Web1.0 notion that emerged in the mid-1990s and has seen a revival in recent years thanks to the explosion in social computing platforms like Twitter, Facebook and Facebook-owned Friendfeed, Posterous, Tumblr, sweetcron, and dozens more. If you're not already familiar with the term *lifestream*, it was first coined by Eric Freeman and David Gelernter at Yale University in 1996 to describe

> A time-ordered stream of documents that functions as a diary of your electronic life; every document you create and every document other people send you is stored in your lifestream. The tail of your stream contains documents from the past (starting with your electronic birth certificate). Moving away from the tail and toward the present, your stream contains more recent documents—papers in progress or new electronic mail; other documents (pictures, correspondence, bills, movies, voice mail, software) are stored in between.[5]

But what began as an approach for creating a living history of *our own* digital lives, a means of aggregating and archiving our electronic breadcrumbs predominantly *for ourselves*, has taken on an added dimension on the social Web. Lifestreaming has evolved into a new form of publishing *for* and sharing *with others*. And it has morphed into a forum for discovering people and content that we may not have otherwise discovered through the traditional model of destination media, as social tools make it possible not only to pull our microcontent together into a unified stream but to quickly and easily push the most interesting bits to our personal networks on the Web. As anyone who spends time on services like Twitter or Facebook knows, our tweetstreams and Facebook news feeds are essentially microbroadcast networks programmed by our friends, the people we follow, and (generally to a far lesser extent) the companies, brands, product marketers, and media outlets we've elected to tune in to. And when the microcontent comes to us at the suggestion of a friend (such as when a contact shares a link on Facebook, Twitter, or Delicious or even through Google Reader) or with a friend's endorsement (a piece of content a contact *likes* on Facebook, or *favorites* on YouTube, Flickr, or elsewhere), we are likely to give that content more weight, to pay it more attention.

All this creates a new marketing imperative and demands a new media model. When a company attempts to interrupt the stream, the stream is bound to shift course or simply flow around the interruption. But if a brand can actually become *part of the stream*, it will be carried along in the flow itself.

In other words, to attract attention, earn impressions, and engage consumers in the age of human-powered distribution, micromarketers—much like the media makers in Jeff Jarvis's vision—must insinuate themselves into the feed, inspiring people to pass their branded content or marketing messages into the always-on stream of programming they're already pushing out to their personal networks and connections. Both MadV and Drew Olanoff successfully insinuated themselves into the flow, stimulating peer-to-peer pass-along of their messages well beyond their own immediate circles of friends. Companies that manage to do the same have an opportunity to stand apart from their competitors and achieve outsized results, but doing so with consistency means approaching the notion of pass-along with a sound strategy rather than just a sense of social serendipity.

SHARE AND SHARE ALIKE

Anyone who tells you there is a tried-and-true formula for achieving (or even predicting) "viral success" is most likely shilling snake oil. Stimulating the person-to-person dissemination of content through social streams and accelerating and amplifying the network effect are far more unpredictable than purchasing impressions on traditional broadcast-style media. What works one day may fail the next, and the so-called best practices we write on Monday must be rewritten on Tuesday. This is why we are so often surprised by runaway online hits and why attempting to manufacture viral content is, generally speaking, a fool's errand.

That said, I would like to put forth one viable approach built upon a combination of three elements that may not work alone but—taken together—increase not only the likelihood of pass-along but also the velocity with which the network effect kicks in and how far it extends. In fact, we can see these factors at play in the cases of MadV and #blamedrewscancer. The three elements are:

- Interest

- Expression

- Motivation

Let's take a deeper look at each of these factors before bringing them to life in a practical micromarketing example.

Interest: We Spread What Interests Us and What We Think Will Interest Others

In the words of Web scholar danah boyd, "People consume content that stimulates their mind and senses. That which angers, excites, energizes, entertains, or otherwise creates an emotional response. This is not always the 'best' content or the most informative content, but that which triggers a reaction."[6] It stands to reason that the attributes that drive people to *consume content* can also motivate people to *share content* with others. In fact, the gold standard for Web content isn't whether we would watch it ourselves but whether we would feel compelled to recommend it to others.

If we are entertained, enlightened, or moved by an experience, we want our friends, other people like us, to share in the experience. This may help explain why content that is inherently stimulating, is ready-made to trigger a response—content that is funny, frightening, surprising, inspiring, immersive, absurd, or offensive—often performs well in a networked media landscape. But with virtually unlimited choice, being interesting is rarely enough to spark and sustain a network effect that delivers sufficient scale. Giving the people that make up the network—the people that feed the stream—an excuse to become more interesting *themselves* greatly increases the likelihood that they'll pass something along.

Expression: We Spread What Allows Us to Share Something about Ourselves

When MadV wanted to make a statement about the state of the world and ordinary people's power to effect change, he didn't simply upload his interpretation but asked the YouTube community to contribute to a crowd-sourced vision for humankind. When Drew Olanoff turned to the social media sphere as both a forum for emotional support during a tough time in his life and a channel for raising awareness of—and money for—cancer research, he didn't simply ask his network to spread the news of *his own battle* with cancer; he asked them to turn his cancer into a scapegoat for even the most minor things that went awry *in their own lives*. The juxtaposition between one man's serious matter and everyone else's trivial annoyances was surprising and noteworthy enough to spark conversation and attention well beyond Drew's personal circle of friends and sphere of influence. When we want other people to *share something about us*, we can greatly accelerate the rate of pass-along when we provide the opportunity and the inspiration necessary to *share something about themselves*.

Motivation: We Spread What We Have Incentive to Share

SocialVibe's Marchese challenges marketers to not only think of networked consumers as micromedia programmers, but actually work with them in ways that are not entirely dissimilar to how they have historically worked with traditional programmers.

"Name a content creator or programmer that doesn't get paid when they insert marketing messages into their lineup," Joe told me during one phone conversation. "If you recognize people's role as programmers, why wouldn't you invest marketing dollars to compensate them for their role in getting the word out? On the social Web, the people who engage with your brand assets and share them with their friends are your message bearers and your media buy."

Incentives might take the form of direct payment in cash or in kind—though these controversial practices blur the line between medium and message and can strain the boundaries of consumer credibility, and for these reasons have been regulated by the Federal Trade Commission in the United States. Or as in the case of #blamedrewscancer, the incentives may lie in both the innate human desire to be part of something bigger than oneself and the opportunity to support a worthy cause by contributing either directly or indirectly to a charitable fund-raising drive.

But social currency and increased social status often have at least as much potential to motivate. In an age of networked culture, networked media, and distribution through the network effect, the people disseminating good content hold a power similar to that held by traditional distribution channels in the mass media era, even if their reach and sphere of influence are often much smaller.

Networks recognize and reward individuals for sharing. The best microcontent programmers attract audiences, subscribers, fans, and followers. They receive credit and acknowledgment as their microprogramming moves across the social Web. We pay attention to trusted sources when they *like, favorite, share,* or *comment on* other people's items and push them into our streams. We click when the people we follow on Twitter direct us to specific chunks of content by linking to them in their tweets. When we, in turn, retweet a link that appeared in our stream, we don't just acknowledge the content creator ("interesting post by @gregverdino") but also the person who brought the content to our attention ("via @amandagravel"). When a Facebook friend posts a noteworthy bit of microcontent to his or her profile, we both endorse the content and recognize the friend with a like, such as "Greg likes Jane Quigley's link" or "Greg likes Amadeo Plaza's activity." When these simple social activities stream to our own profiles or into our friends' news feeds, the pass-along effect and the role of each person in the chain are made visible to our networks.

Ultimately, when a microprogrammer delivers sufficient value, that microprogrammer earns status within his or her community. The YouTube community members who submitted their segments for MadV's "One World" videos did so knowing that the best clips would be featured in the much-watched final compilations, a form of social currency that has significant value for content creators hoping to make their mark. But MadV himself also earned status as the programmer who mashed up the most affecting user-submitted bits into something worth watching and spreading.

While this may all sound very heady in theory, in practice it can be both simple and effective. Let's look at how one brand marketer applied these exact same principles—the triple threat of interest, expression, and motivation—to tap into the network effect and achieve micromarketing success.

SWEET SUCCESS WITH SOCIAL SHARING

In early 2009, agricultural multinational Cargill introduced Truvia to consumers with a $20 million campaign comprising everything from print, television, and online advertising to in-store promotion and sampling events.[7] Not only was Truvia Cargill's first consumer-facing product (historically, the company provides products and services to food and beverage manufacturers rather than directly to supermarket shoppers themselves); it also marked the company's largest ever push into mass media. The brand's tagline touted the product—an all-natural, calorie-free tabletop sweetener derived from the stevia plant—as "Honestly Sweet," and advertising began appearing in mass media around the same time that consumer packaged goods giants Coca-Cola and Pepsi were making pushes into stevia-sweetened beverages and specialty manufacturer Whole Earth Sweetener was marketing its own stevia-based PureVia product.

But by autumn 2009, Cargill was looking for creative ways to become involved with social networking as a means of engaging new audiences in new ways. The company wanted to forge a simple but powerful association between the Truvia brand and the concept of sweet, not only to reinforce, amplify, and actualize the positioning and messaging presented in the "Honestly Sweet" campaign but also to effectively define (or more precisely, *redefine*) the tabletop sweetener category.

Working with Joe Marchese's company, SocialVibe, the brand conceived an initiative dubbed *My Sweetest Moment*. The program is rooted in a fundamental insight about why people share content with other people, how people pick and choose the selected bits of microcontent that they will incorporate into their personal program lineup in the form of sharing, linking, status updates, and tweets. It is an insight evident in the three-part interest-expression-motivation methodology I've outlined above. As Joe explains it:

> I don't want to share a marketer's message. I want to share
> *my interpretation* of a marketer's message. So people

wouldn't want to pass along messages letting their friends know "Truvia is sweet." It's boring and doesn't work as programming. But what if we let people share *their sweetest moment*, upload a picture of something that means a lot to them personally and easily share it with their friends on Facebook and Twitter? Wouldn't the pass-along rate for *that* content be pretty high? Once you've uploaded your picture, of course you'll want to share it with people—it was *your* sweetest moment. Truvia basically gave people an excuse to share something about themselves, something that might not have otherwise come up in the normal course of online conversation. And the things the people shared absolutely reinforced Truvia's "honestly sweet" positioning and the brand got to ride along with the programming.

In short, while the pass-along effect of more traditional messages—one-way communications transplanted from traditional channels to new ones—might not deliver against marketers' often lofty expectations about viral marketing, personal interpretations of those messages might hold the key to Web-scale distribution.

The photos shared through My Sweetest Moment are honest and personal, are often emotional, and carry the potential to have a strong positive impact on the receiver—my first kiss, my first boyfriend, the first time I held my baby, when my father came home from Iraq, the look of utter joy on my daughter's face as she played with a friend. When someone you know—certainly a true friend, but even a loose tie you've made and fostered over time through the ambient albeit always-on connectivity of social networking—shares these types of intimate moments with you,

you're likely to pay attention. As microcontent goes, little could be more relevant or resonant.

The mechanism for sharing was seamless. Those who uploaded an image were prompted to tweet links to their content—tweets like "Come check out my sweetest moment, with @truvia ... http://bit.ly/3DHLaH #socialvibe"—push an update into their Facebook feed or e-mail the URL to the people in their personal address books. Recipients were prompted not only to view their friend's content but to add comments and, of course, join in by offering up their own sweetest moments.

Consistent with SocialVibe's model, consumer engagements of every type—from uploaded photos, to hashtagged tweets, to presentation of the Truvia-branded asset on the uploaders' social network profiles, to views and comments generated by each shared image—resulted in Cargill-paid microdonations to a number of different charitable causes selected by the consumers who got involved and participated in the program.

With My Sweetest Moment, Truvia effectively combined the three elements of interest, expression, and motivation. The program's emphasis on emotional consumer-uploaded photographs established interest and inspired participants to express themselves by sharing something personal with their friends. The addition of a micro-donation incentive scheme motivated both the participants and the recipients to spread the content and interact with it in simple but meaningful ways.

As social media–centric micromarketing, My Sweetest Moment delivered. When I spoke with Joe in late November 2009, tens-of-thousands of people had uploaded and shared their own sweetest moment photographs, and he estimated that, through the network effect of peer-to-peer distribution, tens of millions of consumers had been exposed to consumer-generated My Sweetest Moment microcontent—all bearing the Truvia logo and messaging, and not so subtly reinforcing the premise that sweet and organic do indeed go hand in hand.

A MILLION TO ONE

The ability to achieve large-scale reach through the network effect is clearly one of micromarketing's guiding principles. Unlike mass marketing that trades on its ability to target mass audiences through traditional media networks, the *networked media* model emphasizes and unleashes the power of the *individual.* Therefore, it is important to remember that each six- or seven-figure audience amassed through micromarketing approaches in general—and network effect marketing in particular—comprises hundreds of thousands or millions of individual-level interactions: lots and lots of one-to-one micro-interactions between one person and another.

In the next chapter, we'll look at the promise and potential of marketing through two-way interactions when one of the people involved represents a brand.

From Interruption to Interactions

Building a Responsive Brand through Human-Scale Connections

"We live in a world where the little things really do matter. Each encounter no matter how brief is a micro interaction which makes a deposit or withdrawal from our rational or emotional subconscious. The sum of these interactions and encounters adds up to how we feel about a particular product, brand or service. Little things. Feelings. They influence our everyday behaviors more than we realize."

—DAVID ARMANO, WWW.DAVIDARMANO.COM

"I've learned that people will forget what you said, people will forget what you did, but people will never forget how you made them feel."

—MAYA ANGELOU

BIG THINGS STAY THE SAME, SMALL THINKING CHANGES THE GAME

In November 2009, a Boston-area marketer, blogger, and college instructor named Zach Braiker[1] invited me to speak with the students taking his social media course at Emerson College. And so it came to pass that on the Tuesday before Thanksgiving, I Skyped into Zach's classroom for a casual conversation that touched on everything from what it's like to consult for some of the biggest companies in the world to how recent graduates can attract potential employers' attention through social media.

During our 30-minute video chat that evening, Zach asked me at what point during my career I stopped being a "digital guy" and became a "social guy." I don't recall my response, but I've been reflecting on his question for a while now. And I suppose I could have answered Zach's query with a question of my own: *was there ever a time when digital wasn't social?*

I'm old enough to remember accessing a clunky, early version of the Web over dial-up with one of the first commercially available Internet software packages, Internet in a Box. I didn't really log on for content (there wasn't much to be had) or commerce (for the most part, nobody was selling much of anything over the Web) or to see what my favorite companies were up to (few, if any, were jumping headlong into the world of online media at that point). Even back then—this would have been 1991 or so—the Internet was mostly about interacting with other people from around the world, with the aid of new networking technologies.

If you accessed the Internet at all back then, you logged on to participate in forums, message boards, or bulletin board systems—to post messages, to read others, to visit and revisit to check out the latest replies. You signed on for conversations with a bunch of your closest strangers in America Online, CompuServe, or Prodigy chat rooms. In fact, if you were a true early adopter, you might have been doing this as early as the 1980s. And if you were *truly* plugged in, you might have joined the WELL,[2] one of the earliest (and today, the longest running) online communities. It was Howard Rheingold's[3] experiences as an active member of the WELL that inspired him to write about "virtual communities" in 1993, long before the advent of modern social networks and even before most people even knew what the Internet was.

As a member of an early virtual community, you got to know some of the more prominent personalities that passed the time at your favorite online haunts—and they got to know you too. You might not have had a formalized list of friends, followers, subscribers, or fans, but you certainly had a network of ambient connections to people you came to know largely (if not exclusively) through your interactions with them on the nascent World Wide Web.

Of course, somewhere between then and now the corporations moved in, turning the first-generation Web into a tawdry

Times Square of brochureware, banner ads, and—a bit later— Flash microsites. *But that isn't where the whole thing started.* As I remember it, it started with people and connections and sharing. The Internet mattered because it fostered lots and lots of one-on-one interactions among people. If you were a digital guy, you were by definition a social guy—even if you didn't yet use the term *social media.*

Without a doubt, the technologies have changed. Dial-up gave way to high-speed broadband, bulletin boards to blogs, chat rooms to presence applications. Today's tools are slicker and sleeker and offer a host of new features. They've entered the mainstream, and the community of people who use the Web to connect and share is much larger and more diverse than it was in the early 1990s. But it really isn't all that different.

So what *is* different? Whereas in the early 1990s corporate interlopers molded the Web into *their* image, today many of them recognize that *they're* the ones who must adapt to the standards of an inherently human-centric Web. But the marketing industry is still nursing a hangover from the decades-old mass-media-meets-interruption binge that is now coming to its end.

Even when Seth Godin familiarized businesspeople with the term *interruption marketing* in his 1999 book *Permission Marketing,* most of us were already well aware of the *concept.* We recognized it in the ads playing between segments of our favorite TV programs, sandwiched between magazine articles, plastered across just about every flat surface, and intermingled with the bills and birthday cards in our mailboxes. Today, we also recognize it in the commercial messages prerolled before Internet videos, spammed into our e-mail inboxes, popped up as unwelcome "welcome" screens when we're trying to access Web pages, and flashing in the top quadrant of our iPhone screens when we're tweeting, locating BrightKite,[4] Foursquare,[5] or Gowalla[6] friends, accessing information, or entertaining ourselves with a bit of casual gaming. We recognize these things for what they are, and as marketers we acknowledge that the people we're trying to reach have never been less receptive, but we still invest a disproportionate amount of our budgets in interruption marketing.

Even though U.S. advertising expenditures dipped by 14.7 percent during the first nine months of 2009 and mass media was bracing for more blows going into 2010—consider Super Bowl stalwart PepsiCo, which in December 2009 announced it would skip its big-game commitment for the first time in 23 years, instead fielding a social media campaign to provide $20 million in funding directly to consumer-proposed philanthropic causes[7]— marketing content still accounted for 43 percent of every prime-time hour according to a report by TNS Media Intelligence.[8] Even on the micropowered social Web—an environment about as advertising unfriendly as any medium or platform can be—the imbalance is no less pronounced. According to Forrester senior analyst Augie Ray, "Social media sites like Facebook are so loaded with ads that a consumer spending 10 minutes on the site might be exposed to as many as 90 easy-to-ignore ads."[9] Seen through that lens, it doesn't appear that we've moved much beyond mass media–era interruption marketing in the years since Seth issued his call to arms.

Even so, long before the arrival of Classmates.com, Friendster, and LinkedIn (and certainly before the masses were on MySpace and our friends were on Facebook), some people already recognized the potential for building business by forging human-scale connections. Back in the heady days of Web 1.0, while Godin was goading marketers to move beyond interruption marketing, a New Yorker named Henry Posner was already putting new marketing principles into practice, actively seeking permission to talk with his online customers, defending and enhancing his employer's reputation through simple human interactions.

HOW TO SHOOT SMALL OBJECTS UP CLOSE

Henry Posner has been vilified as a liar, was once accused of being a con man, and has had his credibility called into question. He has also been told he *rocks*, been likened to Santa Claus, and been praised for his godlike patience. Most of these characterizations seem odd for a sturdy, upstanding middle-aged gentleman who is articulate and mild mannered and tends toward conservative business dress. But it's all in a day's work at B&H Photo-Video, the largest independent photography equipment retailer in the United States, operating out of a single, bustling midtown Manhattan brick-and-mortar location that serves more than 10,000 customers daily.

Henry joined B&H 15 years ago, following a 20-year career as a professional photographer. After a short stint as the store's training manager, he and his boss realized he would be more valuable to the business by serving in a customer-facing position. Soon he was talking to customers every single day, not in the store but from behind a glowing desktop monitor as he made his way through a small handful of early online services.

I first met Henry at a book launch event for David Meerman Scott's *World Wide Rave*, where we both participated in a lively panel discussion about how brands can build massive movements one raving fan at a time. This was in early spring 2009, and the thing that struck me most about Henry was this: while he spoke the language of social *marketing*—listening and response, transparency and authenticity, relationships and conversation—he didn't speak the language of social *media*. He didn't see much point in Twitter (he later joined and now tweets from one of several official B&H Photo-Video accounts); wasn't big on Facebook (he has a personal profile but doesn't manage the official B&H Photo-Video Page); scarcely mentioned blogs, podcasts, YouTube, Flickr, or mobile; and didn't seem to be keeping an eye out for any new media *next big things*.

Follow Henry Posner on Twitter

twitter.com/bandhphoto

To be perfectly clear, Henry is far from a Luddite; he just knows how to keep things in perspective. He knows that social marketing is not about the tools you use, but about what you do with them. If you're looking for proof that micromarketing (or even social media in general) has little to do with technology and everything to do with humanity, Henry's story provides it better than any other example in this book.

For more than a decade, Henry has been doing what many marketers struggle to accomplish even today—sidestepping unwelcome and increasingly ineffective interruption marketing approaches, while using the Internet to build his company's brand through human-to-human microinteractions—using a set of tools, channels, and platforms that existed long before most marketers realized that digital was social all along. In a telephone conversation, Henry recounted the story of how he came to be the online face of B&H Photo-Video:

> When I first started in this role, we didn't know the term *social media*. I just called it my job. I would spend an hour a day in the CompuServe and Prodigy photo forums, mostly looking for places to talk about the equipment we sold and how to use it. This was before I really got involved in a lot of what I do now: a combination of damage control, public relations, and customer support. Pretty soon though, I expanded into the Usenet groups, which is where we really started seeing unvarnished, unbridled, unmoderated comments . . . and where the level of conversation became more direct and assertive. I literally used to print this stuff, highlight the comments I thought were relevant, cross-reference customer complaints with customer orders, and hand it all to my manager. For a long time, this was the only avenue we had for feedback from our customers.

Before long, Henry recognized that the conversations taking place among consumers in forums and groups represented more than just a means of gathering feedback; they provided a new opportunity to establish two-way dialogue between B&H and its buyers. This might seem obvious today, but in an era that predated the arrival of the social Web by at least a few years—when only a small handful of B&H employees even had e-mail and the company's entire Web presence comprised a simple FAQ advising potential customers, "No we don't take American Express"—this insight was groundbreaking. And the fact that a single-store retailer had even a single employee responsible for interacting one-on-one with online consumers was even more so.

Years later, Henry is B&H Photo-Video's director of corporate communications but still spends little of his time issuing announcements, fielding press inquiries, and pitching stories to photography-enthusiast media outlets. He spends the majority of his time actively participating in well over 100 different forums, commenting on blog posts, and interacting with his Twitter community.

"I still go into forums, on blogs, and now on Twitter of course, looking for people talking about the company, what we do, and how we do it. Or talking about the products we sell, what they are, and how to use them. And I try to engage in the conversation positively when I can," he told me, describing his typical day at the office. "A lot of the time, that means helping solve problems with customer orders or answering people's questions about our business policies or how to buy from us." Issues are resolved, questions are answered, advice is offered, suggestions are routed to the appropriate B&H teams, and the best among them shape the way the store conducts its business—all microinteractions that can only happen between two real people and, when done right, can influence the way consumers feel about B&H Photo-Video better than traditional interruption advertising ever could.

A CLEAR FOCUS ON HUMAN-SCALE INTERACTIONS

As Henry Posner speaks about what he does and how he does it, five common themes emerge. In turn, these themes impart a series of simple lessons that can be applied to virtually any business, allowing marketers to build a responsive, responsible brand that connects with people through direct company-to-consumer microinteractions.

Establish a Credible Voice

Interacting at a human scale allows Henry to share his subject-matter expertise and, by association, establish his employer as an authoritative participant instead of an unwelcome interloper. According to Henry, "Because I was a professional photographer for 20 years, I'm in a unique position to talk about the products themselves and specific techniques. I think in some ways this lends credibility and gives me entry into certain forums where I might not otherwise be tolerated."

In human-scale interactions, providing value and proving your worth generally trump traditional *telling and selling*. Every company employs subject-matter experts—whether they work on the marketing communications team, labor within the engineering or product management departments, sit at the help desk, or man phones in the call center. These people should be on the front line, representing their organizations in credible value-oriented consumer interactions. In this case, credibility holds the key to permission in a postinterruption age.

Lend a Helping Hand

A couple of years ago, a *DP Review* member posted to one of the site's forums, looking for advice about how he might get his hands on an a copy of an old B&H invoice for a lens that had recently been stolen while he was traveling. Henry caught his customer's cry for help, matched the man's forum identification to the store's purchase order system, and let the man know he would soon receive the invoice by e-mail. "He thanked me and said he felt foolish for tying up the forum when he should have known to contact me directly. In public I said *you're welcome*, but in private I was thinking *thank you, this is much better*. This way, lots and lots of people saw it and hopefully were impressed with how helpful and responsive we were in this matter."

When positive brand-to-customer interactions occur in public forums, it stands to reason that they will contribute to consumers' favorable perception of the company involved. Of course, it is equally important—if not more critical—to interact directly with unhappy customers and engage in swift, professional damage control when situations arise. This is time-consuming work, requiring far more than the hour per day Henry spent at the outset:

> If a damage control issue crops up in one of the bigger forums I monitor daily—photo specialty sites like FredMiranda.com,[10] *Digital Photography Review*,[11] or Nikonians[12]—I can spend a good portion of my day making sure my replies are current, because the Web is a very immediate environment. If too much time passes after my last contribution and too many comments pile up without my response—well—it's like everyone remembers the headline about the arrest but not the article about the acquittal two years later.

Kiss Your Customers on the Cheek

During the 2009 holiday season, one Twitter user mused that she'd like Santa to bring her "a zombie . . . or maybe just a gift certificate from B&H Photo." When the tweet hit Henry's stream, he took the time to visit the woman's profile, click through to the blog URL included in her Twitter profile information, and match her name to his company's customer database. He couldn't help with the zombie. But after finding that she had purchased products from B&H in the past, he surprised her by mailing a $20 gift certificate as, in Henry's words, "a little kiss on the cheek." She was ecstatic and followed up with three separate thank you tweets to let her 3,000-odd followers know what B&H had done. Each mentioned the camera store's name, referenced Henry's @bandhphoto Twitter handle, and included a #bhphotovideo hashtag.

When a company takes the time and makes the effort, even the simplest things have the potential to *surprise and delight* customers. Children eagerly sift through caramel-covered popcorn and roasted peanuts to find the trinket at the bottom of the Cracker Jack box. Smiles cross the faces of Zappos[13] shoppers when they receive e-mail notifications informing them that their latest order will ship for free. The unexpected gesture, the token of appreciation, the knowing wink, and, of course, something for nothing: they're all simple, small things that might not generate mass awareness or drive measurable lifts in next month's sales figures, but one by one over time they absolutely affect the way people feel about a company, brand, or product. By applying the principle of *surprise and delight* to selected online interactions, businesses have the opportunity to generate goodwill and stimulate positive online word of mouth both on online and off.

Offer Thanks

"I'm very big on finding places where people are mentioning my name in a good way, and just saying *thank you*," Henry explains. "If nothing else, it lets them—and everyone else in the forum thread—know that we're in there too and that their decision to do business with us has not gone unnoticed. I think things like that mean a lot later on if the proverbial you-know-what hits the fan."

Put a Human Face on Your Business

In 1993, the *New Yorker* published a now-iconic single-panel cartoon by Peter Steiner, depicting a black canine sitting in a chair before a computer while a spotted pooch looks up eagerly from the foot of the desk. The first speaks the caption to the second: "On the Internet, nobody knows you're a dog."

See Peter Steiner's Cartoon on Wikipedia

bit.ly/internetdogs

Although Steiner originally insisted he had no profound meaning in mind as he drew the comic, it has since come to symbolize Internet users' ability to interact with one another in relative online anonymity, to represent themselves and see each other in almost any way they choose. And for consumers, this premise still holds true to some extent today; so although the odds are good you know the true names of your Facebook friends,

LinkedIn connections, and even many of the people you follow on Twitter, consider the masked MadV, anonymous blog commenters and in some cases anonymous *bloggers*, or the residents of virtual worlds like Second Life who know one another by assumed names and represent themselves in avatar form. But the opposite is true for corporations.

While companies have historically hidden behind logos, brand names, taglines, and carefully constructed corporate facades, the social Web demands that businesses operate with a new level of authenticity. But it also allows them to resonate with an unprecedented degree of humanity. This, in turn, allows micromarketers like B&H Photo-Video to demonstrate their commitment to customers and prove themselves to be responsible, responsive, and ready to interact.

As Henry describes it, "Now people know that we're a group of real people and not nameless, faceless, anonymous robots. And people know that we don't treat our customers like nameless, faceless anonymous robots either. I want customers to like B&H, to think well of B&H, to recognize that B&H cares about our customers and appreciates the business they bring us. I want them to feel this way because it's true. We do this because we believe in it. We're not rewrapping and regifting last year's tired old goodwill."

THE TIME TO INTERACT IS NOW

While rewrapping and regifting last year's tired old goodwill would be problematic under *any* circumstance, it has become increasingly important that marketers not rewrap and regift *last minute's* goodwill either. Doing the right small things to shift from interruptions to interactions lays the groundwork for making a related—and no less disruptive—shift from marketing in an artificially constructed (and artificially *constricted*) prime time to engaging consumers in real time.

In Chapter 6 we'll build upon the core principles presented in this one, explore a series of micromarketing approaches that tap into and leverage the emergence of the real-time Web, and think about a rising imperative for doing business *in the now*.

6

From Prime Time to Real Time

Making a Real Difference
by Doing Business
at the Speed of Now

"The world is changing very fast. Big will
not beat small anymore. It will be the fast
beating the slow."
—RUPERT MURDOCH

"Speed is a great asset; but it's greater
when it's combined with quickness—and
there's a big difference."
—TY COBB

"Right here, right now, watching the world
wake up from history."
—JESUS JONES

WHAT'S HAPPENING ... RIGHT NOW?

"What's happening?"

This simple question is Twitter's opening gambit.* It's a conversation starter for sure, the first thing members see when they visit the service's Website, an open-ended prompt perched atop an empty text field. The exact phrasing—the use of present tense—is no accident. The question "What's happening?" doesn't ask users to document the past; it asks them to narrate the *now*.

Of course, this question and the mundane slice-of-life responses it elicits might inspire some detractors to respond with an equally blunt "Who cares?" and cause skeptics to wonder if we're wallowing in a never-ending stream of minutiae. Yet as Twitter's community of users will attest, the question and the service aren't nearly as pointless as they might at first seem. Like

---

* The more open-ended "What's happening?" replaced Twitter's original conversation starter "What Are You Doing?" in fall 2009, perhaps as an acknowledgment by the site's designers that people were putting the service to broader use than the founders might have originally anticipated.

so many social computing services before it, Twitter does nothing more than tap into innate human traits (our desire to speak our mind, our interest in others), shifts the resulting behaviors (in this case, small talk) from the kitchen table to the Web, and expands the network of people with whom you can connect beyond the relatively small circle of people you actually know.

The journalist Steven Johnson nailed this point in his June 15, 2009, *Newsweek* cover story:

> Twitter turns out to have unexpected depth. In part this is because hearing about what your friends had for breakfast is actually more interesting than it sounds. The technology writer Clive Thompson calls this "ambient awareness": by following these quick, abbreviated status reports from members of your extended social network, you get a strangely satisfying glimpse of their daily routines. We don't think it at all moronic to start a phone call with a friend by asking how her day is going. Twitter gives you the same information without your even having to ask. The social warmth of all those stray details shouldn't be taken lightly.

Marketers would be foolish to discount the value of social warmth, but—as we saw with #iranelection, #blamedrewscancer, and even #paranormalactivity—it's a mistake to compartmentalize Twitter as nothing more than a fishbowl overflowing with idle chitchat. At the hands of tens of millions of active users, Twitter has become a forum for sharing not only the details of what we happen to be doing, but also a steady stream of updates about what we're thinking, feeling, witnessing, reading, learning about, interested in, and more. And our network of ambient friends responds with all sorts of information, advice, anecdotes, entertainment, and conversation.

While many of the updates that hit a given person's stream *could* fairly be called (in Johnson's words) "stray details," at least a portion of the activity might more accurately be considered *essential details*. Businesses that recognize this key distinction—and also understand that the common saying "time is of the essence" has never held more weight than it does today—have an opportunity to take human-scale interactions (like the ones B&H Photo-Video's Henry Posner has been conducting for years) to the next level.

JUST-IN-TIME ARRIVAL

Winter 2008 was drawing to a close. I was in an Orlando hotel room, awake and showered before sunrise, preparing to fly home to New York from a conference where I had led a marketing workshop. I was feeling pretty good, despite the early hour. The previous day's speaking gig had gone well; I had met some great new people and had gotten plenty of good ideas from the other presenters. Now, I was packed, checked out, and ready to head to the airport with plenty of time to spare.

I scanned the room one last time, making sure I wasn't leaving anything behind, and grabbed my phone off the desk. Just before slipping it into my jeans pocket, I checked for new e-mails and voice mails. Never mind that just about everyone I knew would probably still be asleep; it's a habit formed over years of constant connectivity.

I suppose you might say it was a good thing I checked: I had one new message—an alert from my carrier, JetBlue—informing me that my morning flight to New York was canceled and prompting me to call the airline for more information.

I dialed the toll-free number and went straight into the queue for the next available representative. After a seemingly interminable 20 minutes, an agent came on the line and, after taking my confirmation number and a few personal details, confirmed that my flight had indeed been canceled due to aircraft mechanical issues. She offered to arrange for another flight and promptly placed me on hold. If you're anything more than an occasional traveler, you probably think you've heard this story before. In fact, you've probably had a starring role in it.

But wait. The plot thickens. As I waited for the agent to return with details about alternative flights, I received an e-mail notification from Orbitz, the online travel service I used to book my trip. This notice informed me not only that my JetBlue flight to New York would take off that morning but that it was operating on time.

When the agent returned to the line with a litany of standby options, I informed her about the conflicting information from Orbitz. After an audible flurry of keystrokes and a muttered "Hmmm," she confirmed that the flight had been reinstated and theorized that perhaps (*perhaps*) the ground crew had repaired the problem. She was, however, sorry to inform me that her system now showed a possible weather delay. Odd, given that the weather map in my complimentary copy of *USA Today* showed clear skies up and down the entire Eastern Seaboard.

Are you as confused as I was?

To sum it up, my flight was either canceled or delayed, due to either mechanical issues or an impending storm. Either one, it seemed, would do the trick. Or my flight would take off right on time. I might be landing in New York in just a few hours, or I might be sitting around Orlando International for the rest of the day.

By this point I'd had enough, so I did what any business traveler would do. I vented my frustration on Twitter.

I'll admit I might be risking hyperbole when I suggest that *any* business traveler would turn to Twitter at a time like this. Nonetheless, I had been on Twitter for close to two years and by that point had built up a community several thousand people strong. Even then, a good-sized handful of corporations—from cable providers and automotive manufacturers to technology giants and software start-ups—were experimenting with the microblogging network as a platform for finding and fielding customer service issues faster than the call center could handle phone complaints. I figured my rant would, if nothing else, elicit at least one sympathetic reply from a fellow traveler. In fact it elicited several responses, including one from Morgan Johnston, a corporate communications manager for the airline and the man behind JetBlue's own Twitter presence.

Follow @jetblue on Twitter

www.twitter.com/jetblue

As part of his normal duties, Morgan was monitoring Twitter for mentions of his company's name, and, when he saw trouble brewing, stepped in to offer assistance. Within just a few short minutes of my initial tweet, Morgan engaged me directly, apologized for the confusion, and confirmed that—as reported by Orbitz—my flight to New York would leave Orlando right on schedule.

And it turns out, Morgan was right. I not only got home right on time but, two weeks later, took to the air again. This time I was heading to Las Vegas, Nevada.

AND THAT'S THE WAY IT IS

The International CES, held each January in Las Vegas, is a sprawling see-and-be-seen event that features thousands of exhibitors ranging from the biggest consumer electronics brands to offbeat start-ups that manufacture kitschy gadgets. Even in a down economy it can attract more than 100,000 attendees, including the buyers from every major electronics retailer, and draws a who's who of local, national, and international media companies. In 2009, CES also drew a small army of micromavens—bloggers, video bloggers, podcasters, and lifestreamers—who could be seen roaming the trade show floor, digital cameras in their hands and bulging laptop bags slung over their shoulders.

In one booth, Internet video network Revision3[1] taped an episode of its popular *Tekzilla* show before a live audience. In another, bloggers lounged in leather recliners and availed themselves of free Wi-Fi and power outlets as they posted their thoughts about the most interesting things they had seen at the event. By day, the social media elite rubbed elbows with mainstream media reporters in the pressroom. By night, they partied at invite-only events hosted by Intel, AMD, Lenovo, and Sony.

On the afternoon before the official start of the show, the largest equipment manufacturers hosted their press conferences: high-glitz events during which polished executives walked eager reporters through corporate strategic initiatives and revealed their companies' newest products for the first time. Panasonic's 2009 press conference was a standing-room-only affair, catering to hundreds of journalists from consumer and industry magazines, daily newspapers, and broadcast media. The company's senior leaders unveiled next-generation high-definition televisions, palmtop-sized portable Blu-Ray players, and advanced digital cameras. They spoke of strategic partnerships with Amazon and filmmaker James Cameron, and laid out key initiatives as diverse as their new Living in HD online community and a companywide commitment to eco-consciousness and green manufacturing.

Visit Panasonic's Living in HD Community
www.livinginhd.com

Chris Brogan, a marketing consultant whose highly trafficked personal site consistently ranks among Technorati's top 100 most authoritative blogs, stood at the rear of the room listening intently as the Panasonic executives presented innovation after innovation. His fingers flew across his iPhone's touch screen as he tapped out rough notes and broadcast them to his network of more than 80,000 Twitter followers, a common practice among social media conference attendees known as *live tweeting*:

> Panasonic announces new hd camcorder with 70× optical zoom. #ces09 #lihd

> Panasonic releasing 3 new BluRay players plus integration to Vieracast. Also new portable BluRay player w/Vieracast .#ces09 #lihd

> Amazon video just announced deep integration with Panasonic on their Vieracast platform. 40000 titles. 1 click buy on demand. #ces09 #lihd

---

Read Chris Brogan's Blog

chrisbrogan.com

Chris's use of the #ces09 hashtag extended his potential reach well beyond his own already-large follower community, making it likely that at least some of the Twitterati following the conference goings-on from afar would get a vicarious peek into Panasonic's kick-off event. The #lihd hashtag (short for Living in HD) brought his tweets to the attention of anyone monitoring the stream specifically for mentions of Panasonic's latest product announcements. Taking into account Chris's primary audience and the network effect introduced through hashtagging, this one blogger's feed of press conference dispatches delivered a considerable number of earned media impressions—easily into the hundreds of thousands, if not greater—before the hour-long presentation was even over.

All around him, traditional journalists jotted their own notes in old-fashioned notebooks, capturing the raw material that would be polished into workmanlike copy and published in newspapers and magazines days, weeks, or even months later. But through dozens of real-time microcontent updates sent while he was still standing in the convention center ballroom, Brogan had scooped them all, making him quite possibly the first person to release details of Panasonic's most advanced products and newest initiatives. What his posts lacked in polish—as sentence fragments riddled with grammatical mistakes and minor factual errors and short on context or analysis, they are more stream of consciousness than legitimate reportage—they more than made up for in immediacy.

As much as my JetBlue customer-care experience illustrates Twitter's power as a real-time support channel, live tweeting is exactly the type of thing microblogging platforms were built for: the rapid dissemination of information to a tuned-in, opted-in, engaged audience. We saw the citizens of Tehran harness Twitter's potential to profound effect with #iranelection, and though hardly as revolutionary, Brogan's ability to tap into the service's strengths and act as a citizen mouthpiece for Panasonic hints at the game-changing impact of the real-time Web for marketers and communicators.

In fact, it was no accident that Chris Brogan was in the room that day. He had traveled to CES courtesy of Panasonic Corporation of North America as part of a program my company had organized to stimulate content creation and social media coverage of the show and (more specifically) Panasonic's own presence there. He and a handful of other bloggers were flown to Las Vegas, outfitted with Panasonic camcorders and digital still cameras, provided with access to experiences previously reserved for professional journalists (a meet and greet with Panasonic's North American chairman, a private dinner with the chief marketing officer, a series of product demonstrations, and, of course, the press conference), and encouraged to document everything they experienced while at the show.

In total, the program resulted in the creation and online distribution of more than 700 discrete pieces of microcontent—ranging from blog posts and short-form video clips to photographs and tweets—that delivered an estimated 2 million earned media impressions and, for what it's worth, garnered Panasonic noteworthy coverage in both *Adweek* and *Advertising Age*.

But in many ways, Brogan's real-time tweeting from the press conference was the game-changing moment, a clear outward indicator that the ways in which we gather, distribute, and consume information—whether it's news, opinion, or in this case brand communications—are evolving at the hands of Web-empowered consumers and prosumers.[2]

Of course, Brogan's outgoing stream of tweets tells only half the story. Just as important—if not more so—his updates sparked real-time online conversation about Panasonic and its products, drawing out the brand's customers, fans, and supporters in a public forum conducive to the spread of peer-to-peer communications. As quickly as he could report the news, the people following his updates responded with everything from questions and requests for additional details, to their own stories about how they use Panasonic products in their own lives. Reactions like:

> **okhumane** @chrisbrogan I personally have a Lumix and LOVE it. Highly recommend. And we take pics of all our shelter animals with a Lumix!

> **catttaylor** @chrisbrogan keep up the updates. Bought my DH a Panasonic plasma TV for our anniversary. Camcorder would be nice.

When Brogan tweeted that James Cameron was using Panasonic gear to shoot *Avatar*—a film that didn't arrive in theaters until almost a full year later—in 3D high definition, one Twitterer pointed out that this was much more than a throwaway factoid: it was a compelling, perception-altering testimonial by one of the biggest names in the entertainment industry:

> **mindofchester** @chrisbrogan James Cameron always wanted to do 3d and was willing to wait till the technology was perfect. Panasonic must be onto something.

As one of the people responsible for putting the brand and the blogger together for CES 2009, I naturally think Panasonic was onto something too—although my own thoughts have nothing to do with high definition. They have *everything* to do with the shift from prime time to real time and a micromarketing imperative to be *in the now*.

A REAL-TIME TWITTER SHOW OF FORCE

As much as Twitter's real-time pulse presents companies with micromarketing opportunities—the ability to engage in meaningful value-based interactions, the ability to leverage speed to market as a means of earning attention and shifting brand perception—it also represents a scalability challenge. A single member of the corporate communications department—or even a small, well-coordinated team—might excel at human-scale interactions but will struggle to meet the demands of a Web-scale community. A single Twitterer might trump traditional distributors and publishers in disseminating information or news as it is announced but can only present a single, personal point of view.

But what if a corporation could go beyond simple tactical tweeting, make real-time value-oriented interactions a cultural imperative, and infuse a micromarketing mindset throughout the entire organization from the executive suite to the feet on the street?

Multinational electronics megaretailer Best Buy hopes to answer these very questions with a bold Twitter-focused knowledge-sharing and customer-contact initiative called *Twelpforce*. In Twelpforce, Best Buy has coordinated the work-related microblogging activities of thousands of employees—executives sitting in corner offices at the company's Minnesota headquarters, sales personnel working out of brick-and-mortar stores, Geek Squad agents making in-home service visits throughout the United States, literally *any and all* employees who would like to take part in the initiative—and empowered them to share their knowledge freely with Twitterers seeking advice, assistance, and recommendations about electronics and home entertainment.[3]

Follow Twelpforce on Twitter
twitter.com/twelpforce

Best Buy's social media manager, John Bernier, believes the program is rooted in the large corporation's culture of innovation and its history of acting small. As John recently told me:

> I think the advantage Best Buy has from a cultural standpoint is that all throughout our history, dating back 41 years or so, we've always been an organization that has believed that we can all be entrepreneurs and be scrappy even though today we're recognized as the largest consumer electronics retailer. We still support ideas that could fundamentally change the way we do business. We're always experimenting.

The company began experimenting with enterprise social media with the 2006 launch of Blue Shirt Nation—a robust internal community that connected employees across hundreds of retail locations and created a forum for interactions, information sharing, and the exchange of ideas—and later built a proprietary employees-only, Yammer-like[4] network dubbed Mix to enable real-time worker-to-worker microsharing. The mid-2009 introduction of Twelpforce—a launch heralded with a television advertising campaign that pointed consumers to the twitter.com/twelpforce profile page rather than to the company's own corporate site—was itself the culmination of more than a year's worth of trials of Twitter as a platform for branded communications.

John explained that—building upon Best Buy's history of social media experimentation—the company didn't just jump on the Twitter bandwagon hoping for a quick uptick in buzz, but instead approached the platform with an eye toward finding an innovative means of solving real customer challenges in a channel-friendly, scalable way:

> Best Buy has been known for finding unique ways to solve customer problems. Although we've made real time the table stakes—if you're going to interact on Twitter you need to play by the Twitter community's rules—Twelpforce is less about we're gonna get back to you within a minute and more about we're going to be where you need us to be ... when you need us to be there. There's a lot to be said about the in-store experience—the touch, the try, the play—but this is about what we can do that is valuable, different, and unique to the Web experience. So Twelpforce is about opening ourselves up and using the Twitter platform to provide solutions for customers that say *look, I really need to bounce something off somebody, and now I can do it on Twitter rather than picking up the phone or walking into a store.*
>
> Lots of companies are offering that type of support now. But I think the difference-maker is that Twelpforce lets you tap into many, many opinions rather than just picking up the phone and getting one opinion, or walking into the store and talking to one employee. You're able to get three or four answers to your question, and that might help you with context or give you another way to think about

something. So real time is important, but it's almost more important that we address the real place. We've made the same type of in-store knowledge available to the customer, but through an entirely different channel and in a way that is uniquely suited to the capabilities of that channel.

It's not just two or three people that everyone's getting the same opinions from. It's literally thousands of people that are addressing customer questions or concerns, each coming to the table with a different point of view about how you can solve a problem even if they're armed with the same information as to how you can resolve the issue.

In practice, the Twelpforce collective offers an average of two replies for every question Twitterers ask, and as writer Brandon Mendelson[5] found when he tested the company's speed of response, those answers come quickly enough to make a difference. Describing his personal interaction with Twelpforce representatives as he attempted to upgrade his laptop's operating system to Microsoft Windows 7, Brandon wrote, "In less than an hour, I received two responses from two Twelpforce agents with accurate information and a URL with further details about the upgrade program."[6]

I had a similar experience myself when, in January 2010, I discovered that a hasty departure from Austin, Texas, put a four-hour plane ride between my Sony Vaio and its power plug. Flustered and frustrated and running low on battery power, I turned to Twitter—much like I had done when facing an uncertain JetBlue flight status a year earlier. This time though, I was looking for help more than I was lodging a complaint—and to be frank, I also figured I had inadvertently concocted a perfect opportunity to put Best Buy's real-time value proposition to the test. I tweeted:

> discovered my laptop and its power supply are presently separated from each other by a 4 hour plane ride. how's *your* day going so far? cc @twelpforce

My tweet hit the stream at 9:06 a.m. Within 30 minutes, I received a reply from Michael A. Sander—a Best Buy employee working at Store #1123 outside Chicago, tweeting from his own account and under the @twelpforce handle—offering practical advice, a helpful link, and an assurance that I could solve my problem easily enough:

> You can use a universal: bit.ly/6dhObm The Targus or Rocketfish brands should work. #twelpforce

---

Follow Best Buy Employee Michael A. Sander

on Twitter

twitter.com/michaelasander

Within the hour I was handing my credit card to the cashier at my local Best Buy, paying for my new Rockfish power adaptor. This is exactly why Best Buy believes an initiative like Twelpforce will deliver a positive return on investment, as more and more moments-long microinteractions between potential customers and already plugged-in employees result in incremental transactions at stores and online.

Over time, this type of near-real-time responsiveness may not only establish Twelpforce as the connected consumer's go-to source for technology advice but also play a key role in driving incremental store traffic and increases in revenue. John Bernier recounts the story of Andy, a manager at one of Best Buy's Dallas-area stores, who used Twitter to provide a potential customer with a straightforward answer to a question about the new Apple MacBook. Finding the response credible and the source trustworthy, the customer chose to purchase his new laptop from Andy's store instead of from another local retailer or directly through Apple. It's a small success to be sure, but as any business knows, individual sale upon individual sale can add up to big results over time.

And according to John, Best Buy is willing to commit the time it takes to turn its experiment in real-time micromarketing into a meaningful driver for its business. "People sometimes ask, *is this Twelpforce thing going to go away? Is this just a campaign?*" John notes and then goes on to say, "The answer is no, it's a contact strategy."

REAL TIME CHANGES EVERYTHING

Considering my time-sensitive interaction with @jetblue, Chris Brogan's CES session for Panasonic, and Best Buy's game-changing Twelpforce customer engagement strategy, there is no denying Twitter's pivotal role in the emergence of a real-time Web. The service established a standard for immediacy, simplicity, and portability by—for all intents and purposes—eliminating the barriers to microcontent creation with its mobile-friendly 140-character size limit. It has provided companies with new sources of revenue, permitted entirely new business models, and even enabled traditional organizations to evolve into real-time micronews agencies. Twitter brought Dell more than $6.5 million in incremental revenue over the course of the company's first two years on the service, the Nashville-based health services provider change:healthcare promises to define any medical term within 60 seconds while offering Twitterati tips for saving money on prescriptions and doctor visits, and the Chicago Mercantile Exchange feeds nearly 800,000 investors' infolust with a steady tweetstream of timely financial and economic links.

See How Dell, change:healthcare and the

CME Use Twitter

dell.com/twitter

twitter.com/askch

twitter.com/cmegroup

But a proper consideration of the real-time Web must take a broader view, looking well beyond Twitter itself to the effect that Twitter's innovations have had on the social media landscape overall. In September 2009, as micromavens and mainstream media reporters were buzzing with Twitter talk and hypothesizing about the *twitterfication* of everything, ReadWriteWeb blogger Marshall Kirkpatrick[7] challenged himself to define the real-time Web in 100 words or less. He wrote:

> The Real-Time Web is a paradigm based on pushing information to users as soon as it's available—instead of requiring

that they or their software check a source periodically for updates. It can be enabled in many different ways and can require a different technical architecture. It's being implemented in social networking, search, news and elsewhere— making those experiences more like Instant Messaging and facilitating unpredictable innovations. Early benefits include increased user engagement ("flow") and decreased server loads, but these are early days. Real-time information delivery will likely become ubiquitous, a requirement for almost any Website or service.[8]

In a comment, *Skype Journal*[9] blogger Phil Wolff[10] offered a complementary definition that builds on Kirkpatrick's largely technology-centric viewpoint and adds a much-needed human core:

> The realtime web is fast, fluid, torrential, and borderless. Fast means your view of the world is always fresh. Fluid means updates come in many droplets more than a few buckets. Torrential because the volume of updates is overwhelming without filters and gatekeepers. Borderless so your information, friends, and experience are with you everywhere online. Realtime web changes how the web feels. More immediate, interpersonal, complete. And human.[11]

Taken together, these two perspectives capture the essence of a shift that is as much about how people interact, express, discover, and share as it is about the evolution of the technologies that keep us connected to one another. The real-time Web *is* the always-on, *forever-now* social stream that brings us a flood of microchunked content, created by masses of communicators and given relevance and resonance by the microprogrammers that filter, contextualize, and populate the flow.

So the real-time Web *isn't just Twitter*, but it is absolutely *influenced by Twitter*. In mid-2009, Facebook became more Twitterlike in its interface to place more emphasis on status updates and make an always up-to-date live feed the central element of the on-site experience. MySpace now asks members "what are you doing right now?" while LinkedIn allows business colleagues to share and see network updates posted from within the community or from their Twitter accounts. With Wave, Google offered a potentially game-changing—if overly complex—platform for real-time collaboration among users. With Buzz (arguably a light version of Wave and flawed in its own ways), the search giant allows Gmail users to aggregate status updates and social activity streams inside their Web mailbox as a means of providing the hyperconnected with a single consolidated view of their friends' latest activities—tweets, status messages posted to popular social networks, microcontent such as photos and videos, and more—and the peer-to-peer conversations going on around those updates.

Looking at search engines specifically, both Google and Bing began factoring tweets and Facebook status updates into query results, while search start-ups like OneRiot,[12] Topsy,[13] and Collecta[14] launched with a laser focus on serving data harvested specifically from the real-time Web. Consumers win, because the engines return more recent, relevant, actionable results. Savvy marketers win when they recognize that social engagement is no longer a "nice to have" for companies that are serious about the way their brands are represented in the results for real-time queries.

BrightKite, Foursquare, and Gowalla combine up-to-the-minute updates with geolocation data to let iPhone, Android, and Blackberry users report their current whereabouts to their networks of friends. Yelp[15] and Urbanspoon[16] allow diners to review their meals before they've ordered dessert, Flixster[17] lets moviegoers pick or pan movies from the comfort of their theater seats, and JustBought.it[18] and blippy[19] provide friends with virtual peeks at one another's latest impulse purchases. Web giant Yahoo! even gave Delicious[20] a subtle makeover, transforming it from a social bookmarking service that allows users to save Web links for *later* to a real-time social news site that highlights what's popular on the Web *right now*.

However, just as the real-time revolution isn't limited to Twitter, it also isn't dependent upon (or tied to) a set of discrete social media platforms or distinct mobile phone applications. The shift from prime time to real time literally changes *everything*. And the imperative for companies to conduct business *in the now* pervades all digital media and marketing. Even a medium as mainstream as Web video—a channel that once represented the disruptive shift from prime-time television to on-demand viewing, and a microcontent building block as basic as the humble YouTube clip—now demands a real-time orientation and an instant-on mindset.

Now let's explore the real-time Web and real-time business from this angle.

REAL-TIME REMIX: ALWAYS ON MEANS INSTANT ON

Instant on is a technical term that refers to a computer system's "ability to boot nearly instantaneously, so one can get online or use a specific application without waiting for a PC's traditional operating system to launch."[21] It's a concept that could be reinterpreted and applied to businesses operating in an always-on environment.

The real-time Web demands that companies boot instantaneously in order to react to negative situations when they arise or capitalize on unexpected new business opportunities. Delays of a couple of days or even a few hours—perfectly reasonable windows under traditional business timelines—today mark the difference between failure and success. Too many corporations learn this lesson the hard way.

In a real-time economy, thinking and acting small means *thinking and acting now*.

THE DOMINO'S EFFECT

On April 13, 2009, a North Carolina Domino's Pizza franchise employee named Kristy Hammonds offered encouragement and blow-by-blow narration as her coworker Michael Setzer put shredded cheese up his nose while preparing a customer's food order. On a lark—perhaps hoping for their shot at Internet fame—the two rogue employees posted a 2½-minute video documenting their antics to YouTube. They—and their employer—got more than they had bargained for. Within days the clip attracted more than 1 million views, inspired more than 200,000 blog posts including a biting exposé on the Consumerist, spawned thousands of YouTube comments from appalled customers, and resulted in a consumer-led hunt that successfully identified the perpetrators and the exact franchise location.

As industry watchers know, online skirmishes have become an almost daily occurrence. In 2009 alone, United Airlines, Nestle, Pepsi, Microsoft, Amazon, and even Facebook found themselves in the social media sphere's crosshairs, scrambling to react as critics attacked their brands with blog posts, tweets, and, in the case of Facebook's misstep, critical posts on the social network's own digital turf. The speed with which word of the Domino's video spread was almost predictable, as was the impact it had on the company's business, and the corporation's by-the-book reaction was equally predictable. This incident clearly demonstrates why a commitment to (and focus on) real-time response is a business-critical marketing trait.

Although the employees were promptly terminated and the video was removed from YouTube within days (at the behest of Ms. Hammonds's attorney actually, rather than at the request of the brand), the company's reputation continued to suffer—even though Domino's response was relatively quick and exhibited at least a basic understanding of social media crisis management; a couple of days after the incident, USA president Patrick Doyle posted a personal albeit clearly scripted video apology, and the brand launched a Twitter presence to offer updates about how it was handling the situation, responding to naysayers, and disseminating positive developments at the company.

In an interview conducted by my colleague Joseph Jaffe for his customer service 2.0 manifesto *Flip the Funnel*, Domino's vice president of communications Tim McIntyre explained that when faced with the rising social media backlash, his company did "something that was virtually unprecedented—having the president of the company create a video in less than 48 hours and posting it on YouTube to address in no uncertain terms that we're taking this hoax very seriously. We used the same medium the video posters did. And yet ... we get criticized for not doing it 'fast enough.' How can you do something that had never been done before, but not do it fast enough?"[22]

While we can debate whether Domino's was really the first corporation to fight social media fire with social media fire on the troublemakers' home turf,* the truth is that two days later is two days too late for response in a real-time world. Although the pizza maker's socially infused crisis management moves might have quelled the spread of the flames within a week or so of the incident, the real damage had already been done.

Following the incident, a Media Curves study by HCD Research found that 65 percent of respondents were less likely to order from Domino's after viewing the offensive video. In its own tracking studies, digital shop Zeta Interactive saw online sentiment about the pizza chain dive from a solid 81 percent positive to a damaging 64 percent negative, while the company's quality ratings in YouGov's BrandIndex fell from positive 5.0 to negative 2.8 in the wake of the video upload.

On an investor call, the company's chairman and CEO David A. Brandon had no choice but to acknowledge that "the unfortunate incident killed our momentum" for a couple of weeks early in 2009's second quarter. Executives pinpointed the video and the resulting negative coverage as key drivers of a 1 to 2 percent decline in same-store sales and a small companywide dip in profits during a quarter for which Domino's had been forecasting a

---

* In a much less high-profile incident a couple of years earlier, blogger and podcaster Christopher S. Penn used YouTube as a channel to criticize Coca-Cola's first foray into the virtual world of Second Life. With my company's counsel, Coca-Cola's Michael Donnelly posted his own YouTube video (and actually redesigned key elements of the Second Life program itself) in response to Penn's criticisms.

modest increase. And according to Tim McIntyre, "Because we were trending positive, all things being equal, that was the one thing we could point to and say that impacted us."

The Domino's incident was unfortunate because it cost the company social capital, customers, and profits. But it's just as unfortunate when companies miss business-building opportunities because of their inability to think and act small, their failure to respond in real time to unexpected *positive* developments in the microcontent space. Let's consider two contrasting examples.

SING A SONG OF SIXPENCE

I'd be shocked if you're not familiar with Susan Boyle, the dowdy middle-aged Scotswoman who took the stage during the third cycle of *Britain's Got Talent* and amazed the celebrity judges, studio audience, and television viewers with her pitch-perfect rendition of the *Les Miserables* torch song, "I Dreamed a Dream." Following Boyle's performance, FreemantleMedia Enterprises—the production company that owns international digital rights to the program—uploaded a video clip to the program's official YouTube channel. A number of unofficial sources did the same, and social media history was made.

Watch Susan Boyle on YouTube
bit.ly/susanboyle-has-talent

According to online video analytics firm Visible Measures, videos of Boyle's performance accrued 47.7 million views and attracted more than 125,000 comments, all within just one week of the original upload. By March 2010, Susan Boyle's rendition of "I Dreamed a Dream" had accumulated 348 million online views and now ranks number 9 on Visible Measures' list of all-time most viewed Web clips. In fact, Boyle's song isn't just one of YouTube's most watched videos; it is widely considered to be one of the most viral pieces of content in the history of the Internet.

Practically overnight, Susan Boyle became an unlikely international singing sensation, *Britain's Got Talent* garnered an unprecedented amount of buzz that went well beyond the reach of its native U.K. broadcast audience, and, according to online measurement service comScore, the performance's runaway popularity may have even been partially responsible for a 15 percent month-over-month rise in total YouTube traffic for April 2009.

And yet none of the corporate stakeholders—not any of the program's three coproduction partners, not the British television network that broadcasts the show, not FreemantleMedia, not even YouTube's parent, Google—translated the video's massive Web-scale audience into revenue. Instead, as the video earned millions upon millions of views, it ran ad-free as the producers and YouTube sat deadlocked in a negotiation over how any potential advertising revenues would be split among the parties. The *Times of London* estimated that just in the days immediately following Boyle's debut, the stakeholders missed out on a $1.87 million windfall.

Today, we know that Boyle's own story had a happy ending. Months later she went on to become a wildly successful recording artist as her debut album of standards and oldies became a runaway hit and set 2009 sales records with more than 1 million units sold within a week of its release in the United States and Britain alone. Of course, *Britain's Got Talent*'s production partners didn't share in her chart-topping success.

The show's failure to capitalize on one of the Web's greatest microcontent successes sounds more like a nightmare than a dream to me. But while you're scratching your head over that one, let's shift our attention from song to dance.

A POCKET FULL OF ROI

When most couples tie the knot, they're more than happy to proceed down the aisle to the majestic if all-too-familiar strains of Wagner's "Bridal Chorus" or Clarke's "Trumpet Voluntary." But I suppose Jill Peterson and Kevin Heinz aren't like most couples. As the 17-person Peterson-Heinz wedding party entered a Minnesota church on June 20, 2009, their friends and relatives were treated not to a stiff-legged march timed to the thrumming of classical strings, but to a surprising and energetic four-minute dance routine choreographed to R&B singer Chris Brown's hit single "Forever."

A month later, the newlyweds uploaded an amateur-shot video of their wedding dance to YouTube and, much to their surprise, found themselves basking in the glow of a global spotlight. Primed by the pure entertainment value of the clip and fueled by a groundswell of online sharing on Twitter, in Facebook news feeds, through instant messages, and over e-mail, "JK Wedding Entrance Dance" was viewed more than 12 million times within just 10 days and landed the wedding party a segment on NBC's

Today Show. As I write this, "JK Wedding Entrance Dance" boasts more than 47 million YouTube views, along with more than 150,000 comments and ratings. With a bit of creativity, a desire to do things their own way, and an impulse to share their content online, Jill and Kevin Heinz made more than just one memory that will last a lifetime. But they aren't the real winners here—Chris Brown and Sony's Zomba Label Group are.

Watch the JK Wedding Entrance on YouTube
bit.ly/jkweddingentrance

"Forever"—which features the lyric "double your pleasure, double your fun" and, interestingly enough, was originally recorded as a jingle for the Wrigley Company's Doublemint brand—was already more than a year old when Jill and Kevin said "I do." Although the track had already been propelled onto the Billboard charts by strong sales at the time of its release, it (not to mention Chris Brown's career) lost momentum when the 19-year-old singer was arrested on charges of domestic violence in February 2009. Criminal charges were, of course, more than just a marketing challenge for Zomba and its fresh-faced young star, but the label saw the JK video as a marketing opportunity. And unlike FreemantleMedia and the producers of *Britain's Got Talent*, Zomba acted quickly to capitalize on it.

As soon as the "JK Wedding Entrance Dance" video began to gain viral traction, the song's rights holders employed YouTube's built-in content management tools to overlay click-to-buy links on top of the clip, encouraging viewers to purchase the track on iTunes or Amazon. In an article posted on the Official Google Blog just after the Heinzes boogied their way to Internet fame, YouTube's Chris LaRosa and Ali Sandler described the resulting lifts in interest, engagement, and, most important, sales:

> Searches for "Chris Brown Forever" on YouTube have sky-rocketed, making it one of the most popular queries on the site ... This traffic is also very engaged—the click-through rate (CTR) on the "JK Wedding Entrance" video is 2× the average of other Click-to-Buy overlays on the site. And this newfound interest in downloading "Forever" goes beyond the viral video itself: "JK Wedding Entrance" also appears to have influenced the official "Forever" music video, which saw its Click-to-Buy CTR increase by 2.5× in the last week ... Over a year after its release, Chris Brown's "Forever" has again rocketed up the charts, reaching as high as #4 on the iTunes singles chart and #3 on Amazon's best selling MP3 list.

Susan Boyle's *Britain's Got Talent* performance and the "JK Wedding Dance" were two of 2009's most successful Internet memes, both capturing the attention of online consumers, spreading quickly from person to person, and attaining massive global reach. In a post–prime-time world, the runaway Web phenomenon is the new blockbuster hit, but only marketers who understand that the Web is evolving into a real-time environment—only companies that do business at the speed of now—will be able to tap into the power of next-generation blockbusters when they arrive unexpectedly.

FIVE REAL-TIME LESSONS FOR microMARKETERS

Over the course of this chapter so far, we have taken a pretty wide-ranging tour of the emerging real-time Web. We've explored some of the ways JetBlue, Panasonic, Best Buy, and Zomba have employed real-time marketing and consumer engagement approaches to address a variety of different business objectives. Even when these strategies were made to scale (as in the case of Best Buy's Twelpforce) or activated mass reach through a ground-swell of real-time participation (as in the cases of Chris Brogan's CES tweets and the "JK Wedding Entrance Dance" video), the approaches themselves were built upon inherently micro building blocks: meaningful, impactful person-to-person interactions.

Let's summarize a handful of key real-time business take-aways that can inform your micromarketing strategy and provide the basis for a wide variety of tactics.

- *Real time is a pervasive shift* that is redefining the social Web, both empowering people to connect with one another in new ways and with increased time sensitivity, and imposing a new level of urgency on businesses that hope to thrive in the now.

- Marketers have an unprecedented opportunity to tune into always-on conversations, shift perception, solve customer challenges, and foster stronger brand-to-consumer relationships through *real-time human-scale interactions.*

- By making *real-time response* a pervasive mindset and cultural imperative, companies can translate hundreds, thousands, or millions of these human-scale interactions into a broad-based approach for engaging and influencing a community of Web-scale proportions.

➡ Microcontent is social currency. The friction-free *real-time dissemination* of news and information disrupts traditional publishing schedules, renders the notion of a wait-to-see prime time obsolete, and provides marketers with an opportunity to start and sustain conversations directly with their customers around key announcements, product releases, and brand-relevant events.

➡ Adopting a *real-time mindset* and making effective use of a *real-time tool set* can help companies address social media crises on the one hand, and on the other capitalize upon the business opportunities that arise when fast-moving memes deliver relevant audiences primed for engagement.

NOW ... AND FOREVER

As important as it is to exhibit a *right-now* orientation, the effectiveness of micromarketing approaches can only be strengthened by an ongoing commitment to long-term relationship building. In other words, micromarketing is—at its core—an evolution of relationship marketing. In Chapter 7, we will look specifically at the shift away from mass marketing's emphasis on low-quality, unqualified reach and toward a microfocus on forging deep relationships with a small but potent core of the right people.

7

From Reach to Relationships

Activating the Many by Resonating with the Right Few

"To be successful, you have to be able to relate to people; they have to be satisfied with your personality to be able to do business with you and to build a relationship with mutual trust."
—George H. Ross

"The only way a relationship will last is if you see your relationship as a place that you go to give, and not a place that you go to take."
—Anthony Robbins

STEP OFF THE SCALE

Facebook has more members than the United States has people. According to Experian's Hitwise measurement service, it was also the Web's most visited destination on Christmas Day 2009, again just one week later on New Year's Day 2010 and once more in March 2010, drawing more traffic than even Google during those time periods. If you peruse comScore's ranking of the top 50 U.S. Web properties for any given month, you're likely to find not only Facebook but also YouTube (as part of Google Sites), MySpace (as a key component of Fox Interactive Media), Wikipedia, WordPress, Technorati, and LinkedIn nestled among the list. Twitter may not make comScore's list yet, but its explosive year-over-year growth has turned it from a virtually unknown upstart in 2008 into a micromedia juggernaut that everyone from newscasters and Hollywood celebrities to marketing directors and housewives was buzzing about (almost to a fault) in 2009 and 2010.

In stark contrast to the situation just a few short years ago, social media today has scale. In theory at least, by marketing on social sites (more precisely, by *advertising* on social sites) brands can reach millions and millions of people with exactly the same message, over a short, clearly defined time frame. It's a model that looks similar to the traditional mass media approaches we've followed for decades, and even on new media platforms, it's a model that marketers can easily replicate time and time again. Unfortunately, it's also the *wrong* model for engaging consumers in an age defined by microcontent and microcultures, in which messages spread through many-to-many networked distribution and perceptions shift over the course of numerous real-time human-scale interactions.

Facebook's nation-sized population or even the raw number of fans your brand has accumulated doesn't matter nearly as much as the smaller subset of people you actually interact with, the people who are engaged enough to share you in their streams. Likewise, millions upon millions of Twitter profiles and your total follower count don't matter as much as the strength of your ties with the core of your community—the people that connect with you in two-way 140-character conversations, the Twitterati that reply to your questions, respond to your links, and retweet your content to their own networks. As the old saying goes, *it's not the size of the boat but the motion in the ocean.*

Blogging pioneer and technology executive Anil Dash (you met him in Chapter 1) learned this lesson when, over the course of the last few months of 2009, his Twitter follower count soared from several thousand to several *hundred* thousand people after Twitter placed him on its highly visible, but also highly controversial, list of suggested users. The list is ostensibly designed to aid new Twitterers in populating their streams with interesting microcontent and generally includes a hodgepodge mix of big brands, celebrities, mainstream media feeds, and notable Internet personalities. Twitter's de facto endorsement can drive suggested users' follower counts into the high six and seven figures. In fact, based on Anil's analysis of the Twitter network, placement on the suggested user list might be one of the *only* ways to amass such a large following: for example, both Ashton Kutcher (the first individual to top 1 million followers) and JetBlue (the first company to reach the same milestone) were—and remain as of this writing—on the list. Landing on the list is undoubtedly a mind-blowing experience for a regular person and would seem to be the holy grail for a big brand looking to achieve social media scale, but the real impact is far less certain.

See Twitter's Suggested User List

twitter.com/invitations/suggestions

As a social media veteran, Anil had every reason to expect that the level of his community's engagement would rise in direct proportion to the size of that community. For most bloggers, the larger their readerships and subscriber bases become, the greater the number of comments they receive, the more links they attract from other blogs, and the more people share their content in their own Twitter streams and on their own Facebook walls. But Anil's expectations were dashed (pun intended) when he discovered that "being on Twitter's suggested user list makes no appreciable difference in the amount of retweets, replies, or clicks that I get," that "being on the list just adds followers [that] don't form real relationships or respond ... like 'normal' followers do," and that the resulting bulked-up mass of unengaged followers "might not actually be paying attention at all."[1] Replace Twitter with the name of just about any other social network, and both the pattern and Anil's insights will still hold true.

In one blog post, Anil drew clear parallels between the flawed focus on social media scale and the false assumptions that underlie the traditional media and mass advertising industries—that possible exposures to theoretical eyeballs are enough:

> It's a bit like when I worked at a newspaper: every reporter thought "Well, our circulation is a million copies, that must mean a million people read my column." Facing the reality that only 10,000 of those people read the column, or that perhaps only 1,000 of them were reading the advertisement on the opposite page, forced a useful and important reckoning into some false assumptions that were underpinning that industry's workings.[2]

By focusing on reach first, all we are doing is re-creating old media's flawed models in a new media landscape. It's a botched approach I often refer to as *0.2 marketing for a 2.0 world*, and in this chapter we will flip the traditional notion of reach on its head.

REACH IS THE RESULT

With the numbers in Anil's example as a point of reference, mass marketers might ultimately measure their success based on the 1,000 people who actually paid attention or took action, but when they make their media buys, they're paying for the mostly indifferent 1 million subscribers. Web marketers (and more than a few social media mavens) fixate on total number of opted-in but unengaged Facebook fans, Twitter followers, MySpace friends, and YouTube subscribers when they should be looking for ways to strengthen their ties with the smaller core of connections that care. In shifting our emphasis from mass (the raw tonnage of social media's scale) to micro (our ability to engage an active and interested few), we can begin to recognize the potential of some new approaches.

What if instead of buying the many to reach the few, we built relationships with the few to attract the many? What if instead of viewing reach as a starting requirement, we saw it as the result of getting consumer relationships right?

People don't love brands just because the companies that bring them to market have achieved shallow reach of a mass audience; they generally don't buy products just because all their friends and family happen to have seen the same spray-and-pray interruption marketing messages. While I believe this has always been the case, it has never been truer than it is today. In fact, it's the companies that do that—and only that—that consumers find easiest to ignore amid unlimited choice and unlimited clutter. Reach (and its close companion *scale*) measures breadth when, as marketers, we should be focused on achieving and measuring *depth*.

People pay the most attention to the companies that make the most meaningful connections with them, not as demographic audiences or broadly defined market segments but *as individuals*. The ability to have deep, lengthy, rich engagements with a relatively small audience is a key differentiator for social marketers, micromarketers, and engaged companies. But unlike advertising impressions, these types of engagements are hard to come by, prove difficult to replicate, and generally require us to think in terms of growing relationships (real, meaningful relationships between a company and its customers instead of simple message exposures) over time, rather than in terms of buying big, blockbuster reach right now.

CAN YOU RELATE?

The idea that the relationships between an organization and its constituents are important and must be nurtured isn't new per se. *Relationship marketing* emerged in the 1980s as an outgrowth of direct marketing, placing an emphasis on building a "long-term and mutually beneficial arrangement wherein both the buyer and seller focus on value enhancement with the goal of providing a more satisfying exchange. This approach attempts to transcend the simple purchase-exchange process with a customer to make more meaningful and richer contact by providing a more holistic, personalized purchase, and use the consumption experience to create stronger ties."[3]

Although this decades-old interpretation of the marketer-to-market relationship is generally rooted in a pretty narrow definition of the *public*—CRM practitioners often focus primarily on the people who do business with their company today, with a strong emphasis on the proverbial top 20 percent that drive 80 percent of that company's revenue—it does recognize the move beyond money toward meaning. It hints at the premise that a simple economic arrangement represents only the most basic form of relationship—and perhaps the least valuable over the long term—that a company can build with a consumer.

In 1999, the Institute for Public Relations published a white paper by Dr. James E. Grunig and Dr. Linda Childers Hon in which the two university professors took a broader view of building brands by building relationships. The researchers—along with a small team of academic collaborators and working PR practitioners—laid out a robust framework for thinking about and measuring the strength of the relationships between an organization and the public. In their framework, Grunig and Hon made a clear distinction between two forms of relationship: *exchange* and *communal*, with the latter being arguably more important than the former. As described by Dr. Walter K. Lindemann in his "Overview" to the Grunig and Hon report:

➡ **Exchange Relationship**—In an exchange relationship, one party gives benefits to the other only because the other has provided benefits in the past or is expected to do so in the future.

➡ **Communal Relationship**—In a communal relationship, both parties provide benefits to the other because they are concerned for the welfare of the other—even when they get nothing in return. For most public relations activities, developing communal relationships with key constituencies is much more important to achieve than would be developing exchange relationships.[4]

You might say that the difference between an exchange relationship and a communal relationship is akin to the difference between simply doing business with a company—conducting a simple exchange of your money for the company's product or service—and being a passionate advocate for a brand you believe in. The latter and the former certainly aren't mutually exclusive, but the two are not necessarily one and the same. While both exchange and communal relationships create customers and even *enthusiasts*, only communal relationships have the power to create *evangelists*.

But what factors enable marketers to take consumers from enthusiasm to evangelism? In their guidelines, Grunig and Hon point to four additional components of organization-to-public relationships that must be achieved to a greater degree if a company hopes to transcend the simple exchange and forge deeper, more meaningful ties to its consumers. Again quoting from Dr. Lindemann's summary of Grunig and Hon's work, these four additional factors are:

- **Control Mutuality**. The degree to which parties agree on who has the rightful power to influence one another. Although some imbalance is natural, stable relationships require that organizations and publics each have some control over the other.

- **Trust**. One party's level of confidence in and willingness to open oneself to the other party. There are three dimensions to trust: *integrity*: the belief that an organization is fair and just ... *dependability*: the belief that an organization will do what it says it will do ... and *competence*: the belief that an organization has the ability to do what it says it will do.

➡ **Satisfaction.** The extent to which each party feels favorably toward the other because positive expectations about the relationship are reinforced. A satisfying relationship is one in which the benefits outweigh the costs.

➡ **Commitment.** The extent to which each party believes and feels that the relationship is worth spending energy to maintain and promote.

The factors of *control mutuality, trust, satisfaction,* and *commitment* will seem familiar to anyone in a happy marriage, will ring a bell among seasoned PR practitioners, and will provide a useful framework for micromarketers making the shift from reach to relationships (in general, and communal relationships in particular).

But as a company, how do you know when you've gotten it right? It's actually quite simple: your customers will let you know. And with the tools of microcontent creation at their disposal, they're likely to let their personal networks and online communities know too. Let's take a look at what I mean.

THE HIGH DEFINITION OF COMMITMENT

In 2008, Panasonic Corporation of North America began its own experiment in relationship building, accepting applications from real families throughout the United States interested in *living in high definition.** Each selected family—just a couple of dozen

---

* While my company did not conceive the original program, we later became involved in the family selection process and conceived and managed the online community components of the program (hubbed at LivingInHD.com and implemented across popular mainstream social networks like Facebook, Twitter, Flickr, and YouTube).

families at first, but growing to 100 households by mid-2010—received a complete, professionally installed suite of state-of-the-art consumer electronics. In return, these families provided firsthand feedback about the equipment, were asked to create a certain amount of content to document their experiences in using it, and would ultimately form the enthusiasts-turned-evangelists core of a Living in HD online community built to attract potential Panasonic customers and support existing HD equipment owners. Using Grunig and Hon's framework, the arrangements between the manufacturer and the families might appear to fit the *exchange relationship* mode perfectly: feedback and a baseline level of ongoing participation in exchange for the gift of gear.

Over time though, the nature of these company-to-consumer relationships evolved into *communal commitments*, with the most passionate families becoming raving fans as the corporation demonstrated over time its own commitment to the welfare of the participating families. I can't think of a better way to bring this example to life than to reproduce a post from the personal blog maintained by one LiHD family: the Calandros. This post—written by John Calandro to commemorate the one-year anniversary of his family's involvement with Panasonic's Living in HD program—charts a course from simple exchange, to meaningful engagement, to infectious enthusiasm and fervent evangelism.

As you read this open letter to Panasonic, imagine the impact it might have on a prospective customer who lands on the Calandros' blog through a Google search for *Panasonic*, one of its brand names, or any number of unbranded product or lifestyle terms—anything from *HDTV* to *home entertainment* to *family time*. Imagine how this one customer, John Calandro, and his personal account of how his family's life has been positively changed by their direct, commitment-based relationship with the corporation might at least begin the process of creating other Panasonic customers.

> Dear Panasonic,
>
> One year ago today, our family was at home watching the installers put in our new Panasonic equipment that we were chosen to receive through the Living in HD program. I'll admit that my primary motivation was to get some really cool equipment, and that I knew our family would enjoy it, but I really didn't think that "living in HD" would be any different from living in Standard Definition. We were already an active family. We already used technology.
>
> I was so wrong.
>
> When we were selected to go to the Consumer Electronics Show in Las Vegas to represent the LiHD families, we had the good fortune of hearing both Yoshi Yamada, Chairman of Panasonic North America, and Bob Greenberg, Vice President of Corporate Brand Marketing, speak about why they started this program. They wanted to know how real families used your products. They wanted to know what was working and what wasn't. Most of all, however, they wanted the technology to enhance and improve the lives of families.
>
> Guess what? It worked! One year later, our lives are drastically different than they were one year ago. We have connected with our family and friends by sharing pictures and videos via email, the LiHD website, and social media sites. We always have a camera with us, shoot more video

than we ever did in all of our years with our old video camera, and we actually watch the video we shoot because it is ridiculously easy to do. Our friends love to watch YouTube via the VieraCast and we love to play video games on a TV large enough for everyone to see.

We have gotten to travel to tell others how much we love your products. We have met so many wonderful and genuine people in, and connected to, the Panasonic company ... We have connected with other LiHD families ... We have welcomed new LiHD families ... When we find out someone new has won, we are as excited as they are because we know how different and amazing their lives will be ...

My wife, who never spent much time with technology other than a camera, made the decision to jump in to the technological world with both feet. This was both because we now had great equipment and because all of this equipment is so easy to use. She started to connect with others via Twitter ... made videos via Animoto to inspire others to donate to charity, and began to develop friendships with people near and far. She now has a job with MomCentral, working to connect moms with each other online. If it weren't for Panasonic, we never would have had the opportunity to meet [MomCentral CEO] Stacy DeBroff in person, much less be a part of her amazing company! One year ago, my wife had no cell phone, was not that into technology, and certainly wasn't interested in blogging. Now she has her own website ... a job in social media, and we are, today, at a Momblogger's retreat hosted by Activision to launch Tony Hawk's new video game, Tony Hawk's Ride.

Our boys got to meet Tony Hawk and play with him at his offices. We have met moms and kids from all over the country and get to spend time with them. Thanks to Living in HD, our kids are having experiences we didn't even know existed a year ago.

We can definitively say that everything that has happened to us in the past year is because of Panasonic and the Living in HD program. We are so happy to be a part of this. We have embraced the opportunities this technology has brought to our lives and we have found that when we do this, we just find more opportunities.

As a Living in HD family, our lives have become richer, more interesting, easier, and more amazing than ever before. Our products from Panasonic have done so much more than just make our Friday Night Pizza Nights spectacular. Every day we find that if we embrace the technology we have and use it to create and inspire, we open ourselves up to meeting new people and having new and fantastic adventures.

Thank you, Panasonic for choosing us. Thank you for creating products that are outstanding and easy to use. Thank you for knowing long before we did that Living in HD isn't about having a really cool TV. It's about using what you have to the fullest and enhancing your life by connecting to others. It has been an outstanding year—and we realize we are just beginning to scratch the surface of what it means to Live in HD. We can't wait to see what new and amazing adventures this year brings to us!

With endless gratitude,
The Calandro Family
LiHD Family #39

Putting company-to-consumer relationship building at the core of a brand's marketing strategy represents a massive change for any company that has come to rely upon scale-based communications approaches. But Panasonic is not alone, as some of the world's biggest brands have already come to recognize that adapting to this shift and adopting new, relationship-oriented models carries tremendous potential. Looking back at some of the cases we've explored so far:

➡ The Ford Fiesta Movement and Tourism Queensland's Best Job in the World each achieved staggering reach and impressive business results, but at their core built meaningful relationships with carefully selected micromavens.

➡ Coca-Cola's robust Facebook fan community and *Paranormal Activity*'s distinctly micro approach to movie marketing achieved massive organic scale because the companies treated core consumers as partners in joint success, even if the benefits to the consumers don't seem nearly as tangible as the benefits to the business (as appears to be the case with Coke's Facebook Page in particular).

➡ B&H Photo-Video's Henry Posner and Best Buy's Twelpforce tap into the relationship-building effect of human-scale interactions to create goodwill and establish brand preference—engagements that both companies believe will positively impact purchase behavior although they generally happen outside the context of the immediate purchase path.

Micromarketers know that establishing, maintaining, and sustaining even a few right relationships makes brands more resonant; establishes preference, loyalty, and advocacy; and opens the door to new revenue. And in an age of microcontent, micromavens, peer-to-peer networks, and the real-time stream, the right relationships open the door to mass reach, and—done right—can also deliver tangible business results. Let's take a deeper look at how one company, and a big one at that, delivered outsized sales success by sharing control, by establishing trust, satisfaction, and commitment, and by building communal relationships with a handful of Generation C shoppers.

WALMART DOESN'T DISCOUNT THE POWER OF RELATIONSHIPS

Marketers don't get much more mass than Wal-Mart Stores, Inc. Each year, the discount retail giant invests more than half a billion of its own dollars in paid media advertising, while also commanding a healthy slice of its top suppliers' ad budgets for cobranded cooperative ads. Nine out of 10 American families shop there, with a full third of the population stepping inside the stores during any typical week to conduct approximately 140 million transactions. For that matter, 22 percent of Americans personally know someone who works at Walmart or its big-box sister chain, Sam's Club—not surprising given that Walmart is not only one of the largest retailers in the United States but also the country's biggest privately owned employer. While nobody would mistake Walmart for NBC, Yahoo!, or Time Inc., its network of in-store video screens could reasonably be considered one of the world's largest television networks; Walmart.com is consistently among the 50 most visited sites on the Internet according to comScore, and its Sunday print circular is distributed to 86 million households every week.

But when marketing executives at the Bentonville behemoth wanted to teach the social media sphere how to save money and live better, they built relationships with just a dozen carefully chosen female bloggers. It was an unexpected but inspired move.

Anyone even vaguely familiar with Walmart's checkered social media past might argue that the massive discounter could have used a bit of outside assistance. When bloggers discovered in 2006 that a purportedly independent, unbiased blog called *Walmarting Across America* was actually a company-funded fabrication, the brand assumed a starring role in that year's most dramatic social media cautionary tale.[5] It didn't help matters when, in the midst of the fake blog controversy, the retailer's attempt to launch a private label social network for teens (a trite and tightly controlled MySpace clone dubbed *The Hub*) turned out to be a shockingly short-lived branded community misfire.[6] Both efforts bore the hallmarks of traditional big-company thinking and betrayed a might-is-right attitude even toward nontraditional grassroots marketing. Although more recent efforts like the employee-written Check Out blog,[7] a series of Facebook Pages, and a handful of corporate Twitter presences[8] pass the authenticity sniff test, the company knew it had to do something different, disruptive, and definitively micro in order to gain meaningful social marketing traction.

A consumer packaged goods marketing veteran named John Andrews led Walmart's emerging media team at the time.* He

---

* John Andrews left Walmart to head up Collective Bias, a division of MARS Advertising focused on helping retail clients bridge social marketing and shopper marketing (collectivebias.com).

was well aware that an active, organic community of online moms was already blogging and tweeting about family finance, frugality, cost cutting, savings culture, and other topics that aligned well with his company's "Save Money. Live Better." value proposition. He devoured posts on Coupon Cravings, Being Frugal, Geek Mommy, Classy Mommy, Jessica Knows, and a half-dozen other sites, over time getting to know the bloggers who penned the posts and eventually approaching them to be part of a micromarketing initiative that would bring together a dozen or so top-tier micromavens who would partner with the retailer to connect in meaningful ways with women across America. He called the program *Elevenmoms*.[9]

Visit Elevenmoms on the Web

elevenmoms.com

Though small in number, the Elevenmoms group—despite the name, a dozen women participated in the beginning and just over 20 women are involved today—packs quite a punch. Eight of the Elevenmoms rate among Nielsen Online's Power Mom 50,[10] and according to Quantcast, the women's personal blogs reach an aggregated audience of nearly 650,000 consumers. While this number may pale in comparison to 86 million circulars delivered directly into American homes, it is certainly a respectable count, and John contrasts the latter's quantity to the former's quality. Simply put, Walmart's mass marketing programs might reach *more* people, but Elevenmoms is a micromarketing commitment that engages the *right people*. John explains:

> The circulars, the advertising—it's all a shotgun approach, isn't it? You put them out there, but you'll never *really* know who you're reaching or how much attention they're paying. On the flipside, each of the Elevenmoms appeals to a targeted, high quality audience of female shoppers. We know that moms are the decision makers—or at least the key influencers—on roughly 80% of all purchases for the home and family. And the moms that read *these* blogs are already interested in savings culture and trust the bloggers to offer practical tips, useful ideas and—most importantly—honest opinions about everything ... including brands. The environment is perfect for connecting with women in a very real, authentic way and the Elevenmoms are credible enough to convince their communities to consider shopping at their local Walmarts.

Katja Presnal was among the early Elevenmoms group, and she participated in the initiative throughout its first year. She is a Finnish former model turned businesswoman* who lives in New York; abides her passions for design, travel, food, and family; and shares her ideas for how modern moms can live life to the fullest in her Skimbaco Lifestyle blog posts.[11] While she wasn't an expert in saving money, she certainly knew a thing or two

---

* As of this writing, Katja Presnal is employed as community manager for Collective Bias.

about living better, and her family did their grocery shopping at their local Walmart store.

On October 8, 2008, Katja joined a dozen other blogging moms at a Bentonville kickoff event that included executive meet and greets, facility tours, visits with key Walmart suppliers including Coca-Cola and Campbell's, and social activities designed to let the company and its protoconsumers get to know one another better. Being seasoned microcontent creators, the women (including Katja) shared the entire experience—and their unvarnished perspectives on the trip, the program, and the company—in blog posts, Web videos, photos, and tweets. Although the members of the group arrived in Bentonville with mixed opinions of Walmart—opinions that ran the gamut from positive to neutral to negative—they all went home enthusiasts who were prepared to act as evangelists for the retailer. "Elevenmoms was so successful because every woman in the group was a Walmart advocate," Katja told me. "Without true advocacy, it is difficult for the influencers that marketers work with to be credible."

See Some Examples of the Elevenmoms' Microcontent
bit.ly/skimbaco
bit.ly/dates-diapers

The Bentonville visit heralded the proper beginning of long-standing mutually beneficial relationships between the bloggers and the brand, built around intimacy, advocacy, transparency, and trust. With insider views into the retailer's operations and

initiatives—and their resulting ability to share exclusive information, offers, incentives, and deals—the moms' visibility, follow-
ings, and social capital grew. In turn, Walmart benefited from the
moms' authenticity and authority as women's lifestyle influencers, and gained some much needed credibility among social
media–savvy shoppers.

Done right, Elevenmoms would help to further establish
Walmart's micromaven partners as experts in money-saving solutions and lifestyle-enhancing ideas, not as experts in Walmart's
weekly discounts and specials. As John explained his vision to
me, "I never thought of Elevenmoms as a community *about*
Walmart but as a community *fostered by* Walmart. Our job was
to figure out ways to be part of the conversations these women
were already having with their readers, to offer them opportunities, involve them intimately in a variety of different ways, and
then let them decide what to do with it from there."

The moms understood this and responded accordingly. So
did the members of their communities, the women Walmart ultimately hoped to reach through the Elevenmoms. "I only shared
news and campaigns I thought were relevant to my community. I
never forced the message," Katja attests before pointing out,
"Most people were thrilled. The best compliments I received
were from friends who said they didn't hate Walmart anymore.
Because I was part of Elevenmoms, my readers were now more
tuned into what the company had to say."

This is exactly the type of outcome John Andrews was
counting on—shifts in perception and earned attention—but
more than that, he believed his relationship-based micromarketing approach to social media could increase store traffic and
drive revenue. At the end of the day, Walmart is a results-driven

organization, its executives focused squarely on the bottom line. Elevenmoms would be expected to pull its weight relative to other marketing investments. The DVD release of a vampire love story would prove the power of the bloggers Walmart built direct relationships with, and the business value inherent in the tuned-in social media communities that in turn had trust-based relationships with those bloggers.

ELEVENMOMS GUIDE CONSUMERS INTO THE *TWILIGHT* ZONE

Over the past couple of years, Walmart has built a robust business around exclusive entertainment partnerships, locking up distribution of media and coupling new releases with related merchandise not available through other stores. In 2008 the discounter drew in an army of its male constituents to buy AC/DC's *Black Ice*, then repeated the feat in 2009 with KISS's *Sonic Boom*, propelling both classic rock discs into top slots on the Billboard charts. In March 2009, Walmart would appeal to its core female demographic with a special one-disc edition of the *Twilight* DVD not available in other stores.

Having built solid relationships with the Elevenmoms over the previous six months, John Andrews was curious to see whether his investment would yield a disproportionate payoff. Could the megabrand partner with its inner circle of micromavens to successfully engage an audience of mothers with teenage girls, 20- and 30-something female fans of Stephenie Meyer's Twilight Saga novels, and Walmart-shopping vampire aficionados of all ages?

As the release date of for the *Twilight* DVD (March 21, 2009) drew near, Walmart prepared its stores for the highly anticipated video's on-sale date. To attract the popular vampire flick's mostly female fans in droves, the retailer would offer a selection of exclusive *Twilight* merchandise (collectibles, t-shirts, tote bags, and more), run a series of promotional giveaways, and let their buyers get the movie early at special midnight sales events. In a move designed to anchor the release events and stimulate online word of mouth, MomAdvice[12] founder Amy Clark—one of the Elevenmoms—would cohost a live BlogTalkRadio[13] discussion with actor Taylor Lautner (who plays the lycanthropic Jacob Black in the Twilight Saga films) in a special episode of the *Stardish Radio* talk show.

Listen to the Stardish Radio Episode

bit.ly/stardishtwilight

Walmart briefed the rest of the Elevenmoms, encouraging them to be creative in designing their own programs to raise awareness and drive action among the mothers and daughters that constituted their respective online communities. While Walmart defined the strategy, the micromaven moms acted as extensions to the chain's brand marketing team and developed the social media tactics. As John Andrews described it, "They *owned* the program. It was *theirs*." Mass marketers looking for reliable sales results would most likely lean heavily on familiar, proven, accountable channels: paid search advertising, affiliate sales schemes, and offer-intensive online display ads. The Elevenmoms took a decidedly different approach, offering up their own de facto micromedia networks to activate a series of small things that delivered decidedly big results.

From Dates to Diapers blogger Christine Young offered her readers a chance to win a *Twilight* prize package worth $150, while asking them to support a fellow Walmart mom by tuning into Amy's live Webcast. The other moms ran similar promotions, took part in Twitter "viewing parties" and Twitter-based DVD giveaways, embedded Walmart-fed *Twilight* content widgets on their personal sites, and used their social presences—their blogs, their Facebook profiles, their Twitter accounts, and their podcasts—to drive BlogTalkRadio listens and deliver eager buyers to Walmart's online and brick-and-mortar storefronts.

See How One Mom Promoted the *Twilight*
DVD Release
bit.ly/datestodiapers

As the Elevenmoms rallied around the show and the stores—activating their communities and getting the word out to a highly qualified audience of mothers with daughters who very much fit the *Twilighters* mold—the network effect kicked in. More than 200 Web sites and 75 mainstream media outlets picked up news about the upcoming Clark-Lautner *Stardish* episode, driving 38,000 interested consumers to the show's landing page. When Amy Clark and Taylor Lautner hit the digital airwaves a couple of weeks prior to the DVD's on-sale date, 27,000 *Twilight* fans tuned in over the Web and on their mobile phones. *E! Online* columnist Marc Malkin took the opportunity to snag his own impromptu interview with Lautner by calling in during the live show. In the days, weeks, and months following the broadcast, the archived podcast version of the 90-minute show has been downloaded more than 75,000 times. Most important though, the effort generated demand, contributed to a 250 percent spike in Walmart.com traffic, and resulted in the highest number of DVD preorders in the history of the company.

And it all began not with a mass reach advertising push but with a commitment to fostering meaningful relationships with a handful of micromaven moms.

SUPERSIZING CONSUMER RELATIONSHIPS

While micromaven partnerships clearly represent a logical approach for marketers seeking a clear pathway from engaging the few to activating the many, they are by no means the only types of relationships that offer value for brands. And the ranks of proven Generation C content creators aren't the only source for identifying potential partners who hold the key to activating reach.

The right few might be found on forums or message boards, within mass or niche social networks, among the shoppers reviewing your wares (or your competitors' products) on e-commerce sites like Amazon, or offering customer-to-customer support to one another on Get Satisfaction.[14] In fact, marketers

can even gain traction, realize value, and deliver results by forging Elevenmoms-caliber relationships with a micronetwork of
regular people if they harness the power of consumer opinion in
creative ways.

Management guru Peter Drucker once succinctly stated that
"the purpose of business is to create a customer." More recently,
Razorfish's Shiv Singh[15] offered a smart update to Drucker's definition, considering that in the age of social influence marketing
"the purpose of business is to create a customer *who creates*
customers."[16] In other words, marketers must forge relationships
that beget relationships, providing customers with enough meaning and sufficient means to tell their friends, families, and connections all about the companies they love (and the companies
that love them back).

In a program that bears more than a passing resemblance to
Elevenmoms, McDonald's is (as of this writing) two years into a
micromarketing initiative known as the Moms' Quality
Correspondents through which the fast-food giant has built relationships with 11 real women in the United States and Canada.
The women—at present, 6 Americans and 5 Canadians—are all
mothers of school-age children, and many enter the program
understandably skeptical of McDonald's food items as healthy,
nutritious choices for their kids. The company aims to dispel the
moms' concerns by providing an unprecedented level of access
to executives, manufacturing, and processing facilities, and even
the farmers that supply the ingredients that find their way into
the McNuggets, cheeseburgers, and fries. The women, in turn,
are encouraged to blog about their experiences, share their
thoughts in video posts, and document their visits with photographs and tweets.

Visit the McDonald's Moms Online Hubs
bit.ly/mcdonaldsmoms
www.mcdonaldsmoms.ca/

But the difference between Elevenmoms and McDonald's Moms' Quality Correspondents is a big one: the McMoms are not micromavens with their own established social media platforms. They're regular consumers; perhaps because of this distinction (or lack of distinction, depending on your point of view), their voices carry the potential to be incredibly persuasive with *other moms just like me*. McDonald's provides them with the outlets to share their unmoderated opinions—company-branded blogs that aggregate, amplify, and establish audiences for the women's posts and other social content. In turn, McDonald's now has an often-updated, content-rich, search engine–friendly social site that attracts visitors and begins to make a compelling case to other skeptical consumers.

The Canadian program extends the brand-to-consumer relationships through a McMoms community that allows any interested consumer to directly engage, forge online relationships with, learn from, and share opinions and information with the five in-country Quality Correspondents *and one another*. If, through the Moms' Quality Correspondents initiative, McDonald's has made customers of the participating women, it is as authentic consumer message bearers and newly minted evangelists that the women themselves serve their purpose as *customers creating customers*.

Visit the Canadian McMoms Community

www.urbanmoms.ca/moms_quality

Just as marketers can create a win-win value proposition by building and nurturing meaningful relationships between a company and a small set of micromavens or actual customers, marketers will both create value and derive value—shift perceptions, engender loyalty, earn the right to advocacy, and prime the pump for consumer-to-consumer word of mouth—by enabling people to connect with one another.

DID THAT GET YOUR ATTENTION?

It should have. Companies like Panasonic, Walmart, and McDonald's are all learning that relationship-based micromarketing approaches can spark passionate endorsements and vocal advocacy better than traditional interruption advertising–oriented mass marketing approaches can. Providing meaning and value, while building mutual trust and an unprecedented level of commitment between your company and its consumers (often one relationship at a time), is a great way to earn attention among an often distracted and even overwhelmed audience. In Chapter 8, we will consider a variety of other ways in which micromarketers break through and connect with consumers.

8

From Awareness
to Attention

Breakthrough Approaches
for Breaking Through

"In an information-rich world, the wealth
of information means a dearth of
something else: a scarcity of whatever it is
that information consumes. What
information consumes is rather obvious:
it consumes the attention of its recipients.
Hence a wealth of information creates a
poverty of attention and a need to
allocate that attention efficiently among
the overabundance of information
sources that might consume it."
—HERBERT SIMON

"Don't listen to their words, fix your
attention on their deeds."
—ALBERT EINSTEIN

IT'S IMPORTANT TO PAY CLOSE ATTENTION

"Welcome aboard and thanks for flying with us. We're committed to making your flight safe and comfortable. So before we depart, we'll be showing a brief safety presentation. This information can help you if there's an emergency, so it's important to pay close attention ... even if you *are* a frequent flyer."

I assume this announcement sounds familiar to most of you, even if you're only an *occasional* flyer. It—or something a lot like it—precedes the safety announcements on just about every commercial flight. For better or for worse, it captures our attention for the briefest of moments before we tune out the crucial details about fastened seat belts, the operation of oxygen masks, and the locations of the emergency exits, only to return to our conversations, our books, or our newspapers, or make furtive glances at the mobile phones that should be powered off until the pilot lets us know that it is once again safe to use portable electronic devices. I fly a fair bit for business, and I've noticed that this is the general pattern of behavior whether I'm flying American, JetBlue,

Virgin Atlantic, or Delta. In fact, I'm guilty of tuning out the announcements myself.

Yet for some reason, Delta's actual in-flight safety video featuring a spunky, redheaded flight attendant named Kat Lee (but known to her fans—*yes, fans*—as Deltalina for what some see as a vague resemblance to Angelina Jolie) has amassed more than 1.6 million online views since the airline uploaded it to YouTube in February 2008. Although the four-minute video isn't an advertisement by any traditional definition—Deltalina makes no mention of routes, fares, or incentives—the airline's branding is clear throughout, and many of the 1,629 viewer comments recount personal stories about positive Delta experiences, making it not only an effective airline safety resource but also a subtle magnet for organic word-of-mouth marketing.

Watch the Deltalina Video on YouTube
bit.ly/deltalina

While the airline certainly set out to attract an appropriate amount of watchfulness from the passengers on its planes—Kat emerged from Delta's rank and file through an extensive employees-only talent search and audition process, the clip was carefully scripted, and even seemingly spontaneous flourishes like the saucy finger wag that accompanies Kat's admonishment that "smoking is not allowed on board" were carefully rehearsed until they achieved maximum effect[1]—the amount of attention the clip received after being posted, *out of context*, to YouTube owes more to serendipity than strategy. But it worked, even in ways Delta could not have anticipated. Of course, brands often deliberately set out to create microcontent that sparks the network effect and ignites exactly this type of groundswell of attention. While these efforts often fail to deliver the desired results, every now and then they actually do work.

ATTENTION AWESOMENESS

When Samsung wanted to attract the attention of hard-core technology enthusiasts, gadget geeks, and even corporate computing decision makers in the interest of selling their new solid-state drives (SSDs), it too enlisted the help of a cheeky redhead—Paul, the IT manager at the Viral Factory.* The Viral Factory is an award-winning, London-based digital marketing agency with an uncanny knack for getting brands like Diesel, Paramount, Sony, and Unilever's Axe Body Spray noticed (although not necessarily for the right reasons) with its often edgy Web video work. But in Samsung's SSD assignment, the agency faced an altogether different type of challenge: create a sufficiently compelling online video that would attract attention for—and create interest in—an esoteric piece of inside-the-box computer hardware that a relative few would care about and not many more would even understand.

The Viral Factory's solution to the challenge, a single video clip entitled "Samsung SSD Awesomeness," clocks in at just over

---

* www.viralfactory.com disclosure: My company partnered with the Viral Factory on some early social marketing programs for ooVoo, a multiperson online video chat software company.

four minutes and depicts Paul—a British 20-year-old technology maven with decidedly unnatural magenta hair—utilizing an improvised array of 24 Samsung MLC solid-state hard drives "to make the world's most powerful consumer computer." The resulting desktop system delivers against the project's promise: Paul demonstrates his machine's ability to simultaneously run a preposterous number of applications and its astonishing speed even when running notoriously slow processes, and he dramatizes the ability of the drives themselves to operate flawlessly even while withstanding a fair amount of physical abuse (a key benefit of solid-state technology). But in the end, the video amounts to something that is more theoretical than practical, even to professionals working in the depths of a corporate IT department. Though peppered with humor, a casual and deliberately amateur vibe, a bouncy ska soundtrack, and fun stop-motion effects that make for an eminently watchable piece of microcontent, the video is also laden with off-putting technical jargon and addresses a topic that (quite frankly) the average person would most likely never even consider. In the interest of transparency, the first few moments of the clip clearly establish the fact that it is an advertisement. In the interest of engagement and interactivity, the final 10 seconds sprint through step-by-step instructions for anyone interested enough to repeatedly pause playback and jot down the details.

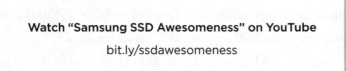

Watch "Samsung SSD Awesomeness" on YouTube
bit.ly/ssdawesomeness

On March 9, 2009, the Viral Factory uploaded "Samsung SSD Awesomeness" to YouTube, and Paul himself—using his online handle *cr3*—posted a teaser message along with the YouTube link to the technology channel of Condé Nast's reddit .com social bookmarking site:

> Hey Reddit—Samsung gave me 24 new SSD drives to play
> with. Want to see what I did?[2]

Despite the ostensibly limited mainstream appeal of a video about computer components, quite a few of the right people *did* want to see what Paul did with the drives. Paul's reddit post—seeded into a relevant forum—spawned a lively dialogue about the project and the merits of the Samsung drives. Within days the video attracted attention from a number of top technology blogs including Gizmodo, Boing Boing, and Chris Pirillo's LockerGnome (all of which wrote about the unique marketing tactic and shared the video with their readers), and by Friday of that week it had amassed more than 1 million YouTube views. As I write this, the video has been watched nearly 3 million times with thousands of viewers leaving comments, and a Google search for the phrase *Samsung SSD Awesomeness* yields more than 1.3 million results pointing to blogs, video-sharing services, and mainstream media coverage. Even more than 12 months after the video was first posted, it still appeared on the first page of Google results for both the generic term *solid-state drive* and its *SSD* abbreviation, providing Samsung's drives with a level of online visibility that most competitive hard-drive products have not attained.

Though the Delta and Samsung examples could not be more different from each other, both companies defied the odds to achieve something that is a critical factor for micromarketing success: they earned—not bought, not begged, not borrowed, but *earned*—attention in an age when attention has become the scarcest currency of all.

But before we dive into a discussion about earned attention, about why it is more important now than ever, and about ways in which micromarketers can achieve it, I'd like to differentiate the concept from the related (and more commonly cited) notion of earned media.

YOU JUST HAVEN'T EARNED IT YET, BABY

In April 2009, during the opening keynote at *Advertising Age*'s Digital Conference, New York–based venture capitalist Fred Wilson dropped a bomb in a room full of Madison Avenue bigwigs. Pointing a finger not only at the rise of social media and the decline of traditional advertising's effectiveness, but also at the faltering economy that has resulted in slashed marketing budgets, Wilson advised an auditorium full of agency and client-side executives that, in order to survive and succeed in the social media age, they must learn to emphasize Twitter over television* and come to focus their energies on earned media over paid media.

If you need a definition, *earned media* refers to any effort by which an organization or individual gains unpaid coverage in mainstream media outlets like television, radio, or print; digital outlets like portals and destination Websites; or social media

---

* Not all that surprising, given that Twitter is one of the start-ups funded by Wilson's Union Square Ventures.

venues like blogs, microblogs, communities, social networks, forums, or podcasts. These media mentions might be earned through public relations programs or just by doing something that garners unsolicited positive word of mouth, but in either case earned media's distinguishing characteristic is that your brand appears in the media without your company writing checks to media sellers. It's an approach that stands in marked contrast to paid media marketing approaches like advertising, sponsorships, and product placements.

Fittingly, the concept of earned media is itself the beneficiary of a considerable amount of earned media: a Google search for *earned media* returns more than 70,000 links to articles, blog posts, and sites that reference the term. Much of the recent conversation focuses not on the decades-old contrast between traditional advertising (paid media) and traditional public relations (earned media.) Instead—perhaps spurred by Fred Wilson's Digital Conference keynote—the writers of many of the posts and articles ponder whether the rises in social media and consumer-to-consumer influence, along with the corresponding faltering of mass media and marketing's effectiveness, have ushered in an age when earned consumer-generated mentions reign supreme over professional paid placements. I believe they have, and this belief is core to the micromarketing mindset.

In fact, the companies and case studies featured throughout this book emphasize earned media over paid media. Some—the Ford Fiesta Movement, Walmart's Elevenmoms, and *Paranormal Activity* among them—earned their media through the incubation of microcontent creation, distribution, and discussion. B&H Photo-Video's use of human-scale interactions and Twelpforce's escalation of that approach into a customer-care program of

Web-scale proportions have helped two very different electronics retailers deliver brand experiences worth talking about.

Others—like Tourism Queensland's Best Job in the World—parlay a relatively modest paid media spend (as you'll recall, just enough for ads in newspaper classified sections and listings on job boards) into massive reach by maximizing an earned media multiplier effect. It's not so different from the multiplier effect that Super Bowl advertisers hope to achieve, sparking positive postgame word of mouth that significantly increases the value derived from their eight-figure investments, turning empty impressions into a lasting impression. Of course, by taking a micro approach, Tourism Queensland achieved an arguably larger multiplier by thinking and acting small than most Super Bowl advertisers achieve by buying big.

Now having said all this—and acknowledging that the distinction between paid media and earned media is an important one—I also believe that the idea of earning media only scratches the surface of the real matter and, upon further reflection, might actually miss the mark by more than a bit. Why? It's because whether you earn your media or buy it, the very concept of media (as we use it in marketing, at least) puts corporations, rather than consumers, at the center of the value equation. Really, the only meaningful difference between paid media and earned media is whether or not the marketer is paying for the privilege of bleating out its message. The two approaches are simply different ways of saying what you want to say, but they are still just ways of *saying*—when what you really want is to be *heard*. As a marketer, you don't want to merely get in front of people. You don't just want to make people aware. You actually want to capture their attention.

Marketers need to focus not on earning *media* but on earning *attention*. Even beyond the reality that people sharing content and ideas with other people is disintermediation more than it is media, this is not merely a semantic argument.

Media conveys—it delivers impressions, reach, share of voice, and awareness. But awareness itself is not enough to drive real business results today, and of course it never was. Awareness is passive, whereas attention is active. Awareness is general and vague; attention is specific and sharply focused. Awareness is seeing and hearing, while attention is watching and listening.

If you said that the awareness generated through media (paid, earned, owned, or otherwise) provides a means of garnering attention, I probably wouldn't argue. But even a means of gaining attention doesn't guarantee you've actually gotten it.

The brutal fact is that, whether your company's message found its way into media by purchase or by persuasion, it has never been easier for consumers to get the content they want without really paying attention to the corporate messages they don't. We all fast-forward past 30-second spots, flip by print ads without a glance, and contract an acute case of banner blindness whenever we surf the Web. We also casually skim the news (often online, increasingly highlighted or curated by our networked connections, and even on microcontent-friendly mobile device screens), picking out only the high points without digesting the details. We glaze over or multitask when the hosts of *Good Morning America*—or even a favorite podcast or Web show—prattle on about some uninteresting topic or another. We cherry-pick choice items out of our social stream based on any combination of factors ranging from who passed it along to what we happen to be doing at any given time. What we have here is a failure to communicate. Or more precisely, *a failure of communications*. In all these instances, we are aware of the media itself (never mind the companies that have paid or earned their way into the media), but it has flat-out failed to earn our attention.

Attention is the scarcest resource. Far scarcer than media inventory or marketing budget, scarcer than the vast and growing storehouse of microcontent, scarcer even than the thinner slice of the microcontent pie that finds its way into our social activity streams. And with scarcity comes value, a fact that has given rise to the notion that the information economy has given way to an *attention economy* in which marketers must grapple with the reality that attention is not only scarce but also fragmented and fractured—much like the micromedia and microcultural landscapes within which consumers and organizations alike now operate.

CONTINUOUS PARTIAL ATTENTION

Linda Stone is a former technology executive who is now widely considered a leading thinker on digital trends. She is perhaps best known for coining the term *continuous partial attention* to describe a set of behaviors that has become the hallmark of living in a hyperconnected, always-on state. Although her original thinking on the topic dates to 1998—well before the emergence of the real-time Web—she continues to explore the trend and its impact today. And the idea of continuous partial attention is more relevant now than ever before. Consider Linda's definition:

> Continuous partial attention describes how many of us use
> our attention today ... To pay continuous partial attention

is to pay partial attention—CONTINUOUSLY. It is motivated by a desire to be a LIVE node on the network. Another
way of saying this is that we want to connect and be connected. We want to effectively scan for opportunity and
optimize for the best opportunities, activities, and contacts,
at any given moment. To be busy, to be connected, is to be
alive, to be recognized, and to matter.[3]

Stone is careful to distinguish constant partial attention from
its cousin multitasking, a behavior that may look outwardly similar but is driven by very different impulses. When we multitask—
eating lunch, while half listening to a conference call, while
scanning our unread e-mails, while reading this book—we generally do so in order to get more done *now*, so that we may do
something else *later*. Multitasking is a reaction to our oversched-
uled lives. Continuous partial attention isn't a reaction; it's
action. It's not a means to an end, but the end itself. It's a deliber-
ate lifestyle choice that people (more of them every day) make in
order to absorb as much as they can, connect in as many ways as
possible, and get the most out of whatever they are experiencing
right now.

In other words, continuous partial attention—and in fact,
continuous partial *everything*, including not only attention to
content but also the loose ties of the many casual contacts and
ambient friendships we maintain through social networks—is
fast becoming the consumer's natural state of being in the era of
the micromaven-fueled, microcontent-filled, microprogrammer-
filtered social stream.

All this begs the question: how does an airline safety video, a
whimsical computer hardware demonstration, or any other piece

of marketer microcontent break through the barrier, earn media impressions (as measured in views), and ultimately grab a slice of active attention (as manifested by interaction, engagement, participation, and person-to-person distribution) from connected consumers? The truth is, there is no easy answer, no formula, no prescription. Consumer attention isn't just fractured and fragmented; it's also fickle. The factors that allow a marketer or content creator to earn a slice of that attention today may fail to do the same tomorrow.

But to get a sense of what some potential key elements—other than serendipity (although this certainly plays a role as well)—might be, we can turn to the story of how one newspaperman turned novelist turned accidental micromarketer defied the odds and achieved surprisingly strong results for some possible answers.

DEAD PRESIDENTS AND BRAIN SPACE

If you think your organization is struggling to stand out among your competitors and earn attention from your constituents, you should try publishing a book. According to Nielsen Bookscan, approximately 1.2 million volumes are in print today, with roughly 173,000 new titles being published each year in the United States alone. While A-list authors—household names like Albom, Brown, King, Koontz, Patterson, Rowling, and Sparks, along with business best sellers like Godin and Gladwell—and their publishers certainly do well, the truth is that 93 percent of all titles published in a given year will sell fewer than 1,000 copies.

Looking at the 1.2 million books in print, the average book sells just 500 copies, while only 2 percent sell more than 5,000 copies, and a whopping 79 percent (that's 950,000 titles) sell fewer than 100 copies. While crammed bookstore shelves and instant access to Amazon's massive database of long tail content are partially to blame,* publishers and authors must also contend with the still-uncertain economics associated with emerging electronic platforms like the Kindle, Nook, and Apple's iPad; the rich multimedia experiences offered by high-definition video, epic films in 3D, and video games; and of course the massive explosion in microcontent choices that perfectly suit our needs, wants, and interests in a continuous partial attention culture. None of this should come as a shock to you since you've made it this far in *this particular book*.

Yet when a journalist named J.C. Hutchins[4] decided to leave his job in the faltering newspaper industry in order to devote his energies to writing the science fiction thriller that had sparked his imagination, he had no idea how challenging it would be to get the attention of the publishing industry, let alone the readers he hoped to entertain. Even if he *was* about to assassinate the president of the United States.

In 2002, J.C. tapped out two short sentences that would kick off *7th Son*, a tense tale of human cloning, government conspiracies, murder, and mayhem.

The president of the United States is dead. He was murdered in the morning sunlight by a four-year-old boy.

---

* In fact, numbers like these embody the notion of the long tail perfectly and typify the state of content creation (even mainstream content creation) in an era of microcontent and microculture.

A couple of years and hundreds of thousands of words later—convinced he had produced a science fiction novel that, despite the odds stacked against it, would find both a publisher and an audience—J.C. set out to sell *7th Son*. "I made the rookie mistake of thinking my brilliance would shine through and someone would print this epic manuscript," J.C. said with just a hint of self-deprecating humor during one of our lively phone conversations. "I must have contacted 60 or 70 agents and didn't even get a bite. By the end of 2005 I figured either something was fundamentally wrong with the book or I just wasn't getting it in front of the right people."

Having reread his manuscript several times over by that point, J.C. remained hopeful that his struggle stemmed more from the latter rather than from the former and decided that it was time to try something different. With no reasonable expectation that his novel would become a *New York Times* best seller by the traditional means anytime in the near future, he found both inspiration and an alternative solution in social media—the very same impetus that prompted his early retirement from journalism after he became convinced that blogs would snuff out his chosen profession.

Already a fan of several podcasts, J.C. found himself seeking out subgenres within the relatively new (but already fragmented and niche-oriented) podcasting microculture when he stumbled upon a batch of aspiring authors releasing audio readings of their own books as free episodes—microchunked and primed for downloading, listening on the go, and even sharing with friends. There, he found not only kindred spirits but also virtual mentors and, ultimately, a supportive community of listeners and friends who would become instrumental to his success.

"Looking at these really inspirational and creative guys who were releasing their stuff for free, I realized, well, if I can't sell it, I'll share it," Hutchins explained to me. He added, "And I really studied what was happening in the space." One podcast novelist had a feedback phone line that let listeners call in their comments, while another read fan e-mails during his show. J.C. thought the former was a great idea for making the community an integral part of each episode, the latter too boring for the audience. Guided by nothing more than personal preference and intuition, he began crafting his own program as a best-of-the-best audio fiction series. He broke his manuscript into consumable bite-sized chunks, began reading it aloud, and applied the simple lessons as he learned them; and in late February 2006, the *7th Son* podcast was born. But my tale isn't so much about how one man created his product, but about how that man *marketed* his product—earned attention, carved out some invaluable "brain space" as J.C. himself calls it, and achieved impressive results—by tapping into the power of small things.

THEY CAME, THEY SHARED, THEY WORE THE T-SHIRTS

If the shift from mass communications to masses of communicators gave rise to the micromaven, and the shift from media networks to the network effect gave rise to the microprogrammer, then the shift to an economy of earned attention has given credence to (if not given rise to) the notion that anyone or anything can be a *microbrand*. This isn't the story of J.C. Hutchins novelist, but the story of J.C. Hutchins microbrand and micromarketer—even if he became a micromarketer out of necessity rather than by design.

"I saw how other podcast novelists promoted their work, took the very best of what they did and funneled it into kind of a bumbling, fumbling, promotional campaign for *my* book," as J.C. recalls it. "I reached out to the influencers of that time and just asked them, *hey, would you play my promo on your show?* It almost seems kind of pedestrian and quaint, but this was how you shook your ass in the podcasting space. It's just that simple."

J.C. viewed the relationships he was building as reciprocal from the start and—espousing a give-and-you-shall-get mind-set—he invited these same influential podcasters (and later in the series, mainstream horror and science fiction entertainers) to make cameo appearances at the beginning of each episode. "This seems like a Kindergarten 101 strategy, but it was positively reve-latory for me at the time: *if I invite them onto my show, they'll get a plug and then they'll promote me on their shows.* Frankly, all of this played an instrumental role in growing the popularity of the book."

The effort paid off, and *7th Son* began to attract an audience that, over time, would grow into a loyal following and base of willing conspirators. This last point is a critical one. For market-ers aiming to achieve outsized results through the power of small things, attracting an audience isn't nearly as important as acti-vating that audience as an army of enthusiasts and evangelists, as participants in the process and partners in success. J.C. Hutchins certainly had a lot of good ideas about how to activate his audience.

Soon fans of the series were donning custom-made individu-
ally numbered *beta clone** t-shirts and uploading their personal
photos to the Web—the t-shirt-wearing Beta Clone Army, as J.C.
calls them, their numbers in the hundreds with each one serving
as an online and real-world *7th Son* brand ambassador. Scores of
other fans, inspired by the fictional world Hutchins brought to
life during the audio shows, became themselves literal cocreators
and figurative inhabitants of *7th Son*'s alternate, near-future reality by creating hundreds of pieces of their own original clone-
related essays, fiction, music, videos, screensavers, desktop
wallpapers, and more.

Where many mainstream media franchises frown upon—if
not outright prosecute against—this type of thing,[†] J.C. not only
encouraged it but enabled and endorsed it. Much of this fan-
made microcontent is aggregated at the Website for the 7th Son
Ministry of Propaganda—also home to a hundreds-strong, vol-
unteer word-of-mouth street team that heeded the author's call
to engage in real-world missions (everything from approaching
reporters at local newspapers to burning episodes onto CD-Rs
and handing them out to friends) designed to stimulate positive
buzz, gain exposure to new audiences, and drive downloads.
There is no surer sign that something (a piece of content, a content creator, a brand, or a business) is not just on the consumer's
radar screen but has actually scored a bull's-eye in the battle for
attention than the moment that the consumer becomes directly,

* A nod to the human clones that play central roles in *7th Son*'s storyline.
† In 2008, for example, the AMC cable network urged Twitter's management team to
suspend a set of consumer-created accounts that were tweeting as characters from the
network's then-new but already popular Mad Men series, until executives from
AMC's digital agency Deep Focus pointed out that these show-inspired, fan-created
extensions into the social media sphere could be an earned media boon.

personally, and concretely involved in the thing itself. In this respect alone, J.C. Hutchins and *7th Son* had already achieved quite a lot.

Visit the 7ᵗʰ Son Ministry of Propaganda
www.ministryofpropagandaonline.com

The story J.C. felt compelled to tell went to market as a series of microcontent dispatches even when no publisher would take the chance of producing it as a mainstream print volume. The micromarketing corollary was that small-scale cross-promotions undertaken in partnership with aligned micromavens, a treasure trove of consumer-created microcontent that complemented the main program, and a flurry of thousands upon thousands of human-scale peer-to-peer interactions between the empowered fan and the potential convert would effectively leverage the asset of attention to achieve the bigger end result of scale. The approach worked.

Today, *7th Son* is considered to be the most popular podcast novel in the history of the medium, and even in late 2009—nearly two years after J.C. posted his final segment to the iTunes store—episodes from the series were still being downloaded an average of 100,000 times each month. "There's this whole business of ROI, where people think you're devaluing your work by giving it away," J.C. told me, before going on to counter this argument with a slightly different view. "My perception is that you are front-loading emotional investment for the end user—maybe even for yourself. Manage your expectations here. Giving something away for free does not ensure it will be a best seller, but giving something away for free absolutely guarantees that this product you're trying to sell is going to get in front of far more people than it ever would if it were just sitting on a shelf in a store."

Fast-forward to October 2009: print copies of the first book based on the podcast series, *7th Son: Descent*, were finally sitting on shelves in stores, after J.C. Hutchins parlayed his social media success into a traditional book deal with mainstream publisher St. Martin's Griffin. When I asked the author how the book was performing as of January 2010, he told me it was "selling better than most similar books," quantifying that by confiding that readers were buying "a couple hundred copies per week." While these numbers are hardly high enough to make J.C. Hutchins a household name across America or around the globe, and aren't even substantial enough to guarantee there would be a second book,* the reality is that *7th Son: Descent* not only sold better than other similar genre novels by midlist authors; it sold more copies in a typical week than nearly 80 percent of books sell during their entire time in print.

INSERT ATTENTION-GRABBING HEADLINE HERE

Now let's explore some of the reasons J.C. Hutchins succeeded in earning *and holding* the attention of his listening community,

---

* In February 2010, J.C. received word that St. Martin's had elected to pass on the sequel to *7th Son: Descent* (see bit.ly/7thsonupdate), although during the tenure of his relationship with the publisher, it did publish a Hutchins-authored supernatural thriller called *Personal Effects: Dark Art.*

consider how some of these same elements might apply to Delta's and Samsung's one-off video success, and think about how even the biggest organizations can benefit from micromarketing like a one-man brand.

Let's focus on five potential attention grabbers: innovation, interjection, inspiration, participation, and recognition. To be clear, these are just my observations. There are undoubtedly countless means of earning attention (in other words, what follows is not a comprehensive list), not all brands that succeed at earning valuable attention necessarily tap into all five factors (in other words, they work well in combination, but each has the potential to stand on its own), and as I wrote earlier in this chapter, the rules for capturing attention change every day. The things that seem to work as I'm writing these words may no longer work when you're reading them, but I suspect at least some of the guiding principles will still hold true.

Innovation: Take an Uncommon Path

Unable to find a traditional publishing deal for his lengthy science fiction novel, J.C. Hutchins microchunked his material, turned it into an audio podcast series, and delivered it directly to people looking for engaging new podiobook content. When Samsung wanted to promote its new solid-state drives, it might have gone the traditional route—dry, speeds-and-feeds–oriented ads in technology magazines or on technology Web sites, pointing interested buyers to dense spec sheets or the cluttered storefronts of online resellers. Instead, Samsung tapped a social marketing agency to produce a quirky video that brought the product's core value propositions to life in a unique and unexpected way.

Social media and the microcontent revolution have resulted in an array of new forms and formats that marketers can use to tell their stories; it's up to us to figure out the best ways to use them to drive business results. While the term *innovation* often conjures images of grand gestures, game-changing moments, and risky bold moves, micromarketing innovation can be the result of even one small step off the beaten path. "Samsung SSD Awesomeness" is one such step; Delta's decision to upload its slightly better than average in-flight safety video to YouTube is another. Sixteen months after Deltalina hit the Web, Air New Zealand took a similar if not riskier approach to airplane safety awareness with an in-flight video that features a cabin crew sporting nothing but body paint in lieu of their regular uniforms. The production is just one element in the airline's Nothing to Hide program—a traditional advertising campaign that aims to combat the practice of competitive carriers to publish low fares and then tack on incremental baggage charges, a practice Air New Zealand doesn't follow; but the three-minute "Bare Essentials of Safety" clip took on a life of its own when the airline uploaded it to YouTube. Watchers have viewed it more than 5 million times (even a related blooper reel has garnered over 600,000 views), and a Google blog search returns more than 3,600 posts, mentions, and embeds.

Watch Bare Essentials of Safety on YouTube

bit.ly/bare-essentials

Interjection: Plant Seeds in Fertile Fields

Of course, even the best content and the most unexpected approaches will fall flat if we do not connect with the right audiences. It is important that micromarketers identify appropriate, noninterruptive ways to add their voices into relevant conversations already taking place among consumers and between consumers and content creators. In order to attract the attention of the existing community of podcast novel listeners, J.C. Hutchins approached more established micromavens with a simple scheme for mutually beneficial cross-promotion. For Samsung, Paul—the Viral Factory's IT manager and star of the video itself—seeded "Samsung SSD Awesomeness" among a core community of die-hard computer enthusiasts with a single, simple post into the technology discussions already taking place on reddit.com.

HubSpot is a Boston-based technology firm that offers businesses a suite of software tools for managing and measuring the effectiveness of content-based inbound marketing and lead generation programs. The firm practices what it preaches with a robust content marketing curriculum of its own—an authoritative blog, free Webinars and written reports, a live Web video series, and even a few stabs at viral video. This approach established HubSpot's credibility as a business that walks its talk and positioned the company and its people as insiders among a community of social media marketing insiders.

Taking it one step further in order to truly capture the attention of marketing decision makers and make the business case for both its suite of services and the use of inbound marketing practices in general, HubSpot began offering a range of free Grader tools—Twitter Grader, Website Grader, Press Release Grader, and Facebook Grader among them—that quickly and easily allow users to understand how effective their current activities are at accomplishing key marketing objectives like establishing authority, credibility, and influence, increasing search engine visibility, and even generating clicks. The tools are fun to use, and some—most notably Twitter Grader—generated a significant amount of chatter and attention as the de facto connected users shared their personal scores with their friends and followers. The results range from reassuring to eye-opening, but either way, they're impossible to ignore; most important from a business perspective, they highlight content marketing challenges that can be addressed and opportunities that can be harnessed with HubSpot's paid software solutions.

See How HubSpot Markets with Content and Tools

blog.hubspot.com

bit.ly/you-oughta-know

grader.com

Inspiration and Participation: Create an Open Loop

Inspiration and participation are two distinct factors, but they're so inextricably related that it makes sense to address them together—beginning with the latter.

It's a simple fact: interaction is impossible to ignore. It encourages people to pay attention and keeps them engaged when they otherwise might have moved on to the next thing in the flow. If Paul's initial Samsung post to reddit.com sparked interest and drove viewership, his continued conversation with reddit community members about the project and the product turned the experience from passive to participatory. So did the Viral Factory's clever trick at the end of the clip—that 10-second sprint through step-by-step instructions for replicating Paul's SSD-based supercomputer that forced interested tinkerers to pause-play-pause-play-repeat the clip as they took notes. In building up the fan base for *7th Son*, J.C. Hutchins provided listeners with a wide variety of ways to participate. If you called in your audio comments, he would play them on the next show. If you purchased and wore one of his t-shirts, he would post your photo to the gallery on his site. The most passionate supporters could become Agents of the Ministry and take more active roles in helping him market the *7th Son* podcast to new audiences.

Once you've earned someone's attention, he or she hardly needs an invitation to participate. Participation is second nature to Generation C; it's core to the social experience and baked into the technology and media platforms in myriad simple ways: comments, ratings, reviews, sharing, liking, linking, and more. But offering willing participants the inspiration to get involved in unique, creative, and engaging ways can lead to stronger bonds and deeper relationships between a company and its constituents. J.C. Hutchins offered inspiration to his Agents of the Ministry by devising a series of grassroots marketing challenges. Similarly, Ford offered its Fiesta agents inspiration through a six-month cycle of content-creation challenges, while Truvia's My Sweetest Moment inspired self-expression with a simple means of sharing personal memories, and MadV did the same by opening up a dialogue about world unity that would only be complete with feedback from thousands of strangers around the globe.

Recognition: We Pay the Most Attention to Those Who Pay Attention to Us

I believe that this is a fundamental truth about human nature and—in an age when marketing is driven less by media and messages and more through humans connecting with humans—it must become a fundamental truth for marketers. When Henry Posner from B&H Photo resolves a customer concern or offers a small gift to a prospect based on nothing more than idle Twitter chatter, these things demonstrate in small but tangible ways that his company is paying attention—and for the person on the receiving end, that is virtually impossible to ignore. When Ford Fiesta agent Jody Gnant says, "I will always love Ford, because Ford loved me first," it really puts a sharp focus on the power of reciprocal attention between an organization and its public.

In the attention economy, it is incumbent upon marketers to find ways of recognizing their consumers, giving them attention. J.C. Hutchins gave his fans an opportunity to hear their voices in an episode, see their pictures in his gallery, and share their original *7th Son*–inspired microcontent on his site. To get a sense of how this type of approach might work for businesses, consider the 9,000-locations-strong coffee-and-cruller giant Dunkin' Donuts. Shortly after launching its corporate Facebook Page, it began inviting (inspiring) enthusiasts to submit photographs of themselves consuming or even just holding the fast-food chain's products. Each week, the company selects a Fan of the Week, whose photo serves as the profile picture for the doughnut restaurant's main Facebook presence. Simple acts of recognition go a long way toward earning the attention from the featured individuals. They also provide a built-in incentive (the "hey ma, look at me" effect) for those individuals to share their involvement with their family, friends, and online connections, becoming enthusiastic ambassadors for the brands involved.

ATTENTION! LOTS MORE SMALL THINGS AHEAD

By this point in the book, we've explored six of the seven shifts from mass marketing to micromarketing. The seventh shift—the shift from hinging success on *the one big thing* to having success through lots and lots of small things—is, in fact, the net effect of getting the first six right. In Chapter 9, we will take a look at how all of this comes together into a unified approach. In Chapter 10, I'll guide you through a series of thought starters that will get you thinking about how you can apply the micromarketing ideas and principles presented throughout this book to deliver results in your own businesses.

From the One Big Thing to the Right Small Things

Creating New Business Opportunities by Marketing to the Power of Small

> "Success in life is founded upon attention to the small things rather than to the large things; to the every day things nearest to us rather than to the things that are remote and uncommon."
> —BOOKER T. WASHINGTON

> "Little by little does the trick."
> —AESOP

WHO EVER SAID MICRO HAS TO MEAN SMALL?

In Chapter 8, I used the term *microbrand* when writing about podcaster and author J.C. Hutchins. I made reference to the notion that today anyone or anything (even a sole individual) can be—or by doing the right things, can become—a microbrand. In 2004, cartoonist,[1] author, and Stormhoek USA[2] chief executive Hugh MacLeod coined the seemingly oxymoronic term *global microbrand* to describe a similar but even more powerful idea. By Hugh's definition, a global microbrand is:

> A small, tiny brand that sells all over the world. The Global Microbrand is nothing new; they've existed for a while long before the internet was invented. Imagine a well-known author or painter, selling his work all over the world. Or a small whisky distillery in Scotland. Or a small cheese maker in rural France, whose produce is exported to Paris, London, Tokyo etc. Ditto with a violin maker in Italy. A classical guitar maker in Spain. Or a small English firm making

$50,000 shotguns. With the internet, of course, a global microbrand is easier to create than ever before.[3]

Creating a global microbrand isn't just easier than it was before the advent of the Web. In these early years of an era optimized for microcultures and increasingly documented through microcontent, it turns out that the concept of the global microbrand—the seemingly humble small business that gets big results by thinking and acting small—not only isn't oxymoronic; it is actually perfectly in synch with the times. And this brings us to the last story I'll tell in this book, a story that ties together the first six shifts we've explored so far. A story that considers how one woman created a powerful—if accidental—personal brand, grew her passion into a global microbrand, and achieved considerable success by tapping into the power of lots and lots of small things. This is the story of Lauren Luke.

CINDERELLA STORY

Lauren Luke is a rather ordinary-looking single mother hailing from a sleepy, waterside town 40 minutes outside Newcastle upon Tyne in northern England. She dropped out of high school when she was 16 and fell into a grueling grind of dead-end jobs to just barely make ends meet. She is also arguably one of the most popular makeup artists of our time, is changing the way millions of women and girls around the world define beauty, and is in the process of turning her one-woman global microbrand into a global cosmetics powerhouse. Her burgeoning beauty business venture includes a Sephora-distributed makeup line, a semiregular slot on QVC, a Hodder & Stoughton beauty tutorial book deal, and even a Nintendo DS game bearing her name and likeness. In a distinctly micro twist, she has YouTube and a legion of loyal Web watchers to thank. But somehow the biggest makeup brands in the world—not L'Oréal, not Revlon, not CoverGirl or MAC—never saw Lauren coming. Her story plays out like a micromarketing fairytale, but before we dive deeper into Lauren's story, we should pause for a moment of reflection.

A full 10 years before makeup kits bearing Lauren Luke's name first started appearing on Sephora shelves, Proctor & Gamble—parent to cosmetic megabrands CoverGirl, Max Factor, and Olay—launched its own experiment in beauty products micromarketing. In September 1999, the packaged goods giant announced it would invest $50 million to launch and support a new line of personalized cosmetics called Reflect, which would be sold directly to online consumers exclusively through an e-commerce site bearing the brand's name. Billed as an "interactive, personalized women's beauty experience," Reflect.com would allow shoppers to mix and match makeup, skin-care, and fragrance products into 50,000 possible custom combinations before ordering their personalized kits replete with their own choice of customized packaging.

It was an ambitious initiative to be sure, but in 2005, after six years of losses, P&G shuttered Reflect.com with a fraction of the fanfare that heralded its launch. By almost any standard, Reflect should have been a runaway success: top-quality name-brand products from one of the world's preeminent manufacturers, the marketing muscle of one of the world's largest and smartest advertisers, a business built upon the late-1990s megatrends of online shopping and mass customization. Still, it failed, and by this point in this book you might already have a few ideas about why that might be the case. Reflect.com's former CEO Ginger Kent theorized, "Maybe it was too far ahead of its time,"[4] although Seth Godin's assessment in *Meatball Sundae* pinpoints the real problem:

> Reflect ... failed because it was run by P&G. America's greatest marketer, the king of advertising and in-store displays, tried to build a mass-market business on top of a micromarket platform. They overstaffed, overplanned, overbuilt, and demanded that consumers respond in a way they expected. P&G jumped in with both feet, swallowing the hype of the moment, and it cost them a fortune.

In stark contrast, Lauren Luke started small: no well-known corporate moniker, no massive investment in infrastructure or marketing, just a knack for applying makeup and a bit of social media know-how born of necessity. Looking for a pathway out of an unsatisfying night job dispatching taxis and into a better life for her son and herself, Lauren turned to her longtime passion for using makeup to create new looks and stumbled upon a Web-ready business model: buy generic, made-in-China cosmetics at rock-bottom prices, bundle them into kits representing specific looks, and resell them on eBay at a healthy markup. Without a brand name to trade on, looking for a gimmick to distinguish her eBay wares from those of dozens of similar online beauty product sellers, she began photographing her products in use on her own face rather than simply posting beauty shots of the palettes.

As her business grew, Lauren found herself receiving and replying to comments and e-mail queries from customers looking to understand how she created some of the looks she showed off in her photographs. She soon realized it would be easier to shoot unvarnished Webcam how-to videos to demonstrate her methods and post those publicly to YouTube rather than continually respond by text over personal e-mail.

If social computing has taught us anything, it is this: we live in a feedback economy in which we pay the most attention to those that pay the most attention to us. As you'll recall, we looked at this factor as one key driver of earned attention in Chapter 8. On her YouTube channel, Lauren provided a catalyst for conversation, opening a two-way dialogue with the hundreds, then thousands, then hundreds of thousands of average women who were encouraged by her refreshing, unorthodox approach to real beauty. And through this dialogue she established ambient but authentic relationships with online friends from around the world. While friendships like these may not strictly adhere to the traditional definition, they were absolutely built on a foundation of familiarity, comfort, openness, honesty, and trust. These rela- tionships—and the attention they earned her—would lay the foundation for what was to come.

In fact, Lauren's videos were soon attracting more attention than her online store did, and her growing base of YouTube friends—many of whom may not even have been aware that her main goal was to grow her fledgling e-commerce business, not to establish herself as an influential makeup artist—started asking her to demonstrate how to create specific looks they had seen elsewhere but couldn't quite replicate themselves. In early 2008, one of the more popular viewer requests involved the striking green smoky eye worn by the R&B singer Leona Lewis in the music video for her hit single "Bleeding Love." Lauren responded with a 10-minute step-by-step video tutorial and posted it to her increasingly popular YouTube channel.

Around that same time, the New York–based marketing innovation agency Anomaly[5] was looking into the idea of developing and marketing a signature fragrance for Lewis. As the Anomaly team did its research about the singer, one executive idly searched YouTube for Lewis's "Bleeding Love." His query returned not just the Leona Lewis music video but also a clip of Lauren Luke applying cosmetics to replicate the singer's eye-catching look. Lauren's tutorial had attracted only a few thousand views. And though the agency executives thought it odd, they didn't give the video much thought until it again popped up in a YouTube search a week later during an Anomaly team meeting in which the executives discussed potential new opportunities. By that time, a mere seven days after they first discovered it, Lauren's eye makeup how-to had received more than a quarter-million views. In fact, Lauren's YouTube channel housed more than 30 different makeup tutorials at that time, and many had amassed several hundred thousand views. She was a true micro-maven with a track record, a following, and a refreshing point of view. In an inspired moment, Anomaly made direct contact with the relatively unknown social media content creator through her personal Facebook profile.

Watch Lauren Luke's "Bleeding Love"
Video on YouTube
bit.ly/laurenluke-bleedinglove

After convincing the skeptical Lauren that Anomaly's inquiry was legitimate, the agency flew her to New York to begin the discussions that led to the 2009 launch of a By Lauren Luke makeup line that is sold both online at ByLaurenLuke.com and in brick-and-mortar Sephora stores throughout the United States and Canada. The Sephora partnership is especially interesting, because although the company operates the number one cosmetics e-commerce site in the world (in terms of both traffic and sales), the heart of a grassroots underdog still beats within the business. Although the largest beauty products manufacturers had been blind to Lauren's grassroots rise to social media prominence, Sephora knew she possessed a tremendous amount of potential, was intrigued by the company Anomaly was codeveloping with her, and wanted in.

July 31, 2009, would mark an important milestone for Sephora, but it would be an even more important date for Lauren and Anomaly—the former planned to open a Times Square megastore in which it would unveil the latter pair's brand-new line of products. Two days before the launch, Lauren and the Anomaly team shot a preview video inside the store, documenting the emotionally charged first moment that Lauren saw the merchandising unit bearing her products and the end cap bearing her likeness. She shared the clip on YouTube "not because I want people to see how amazing this is for me," as Lauren herself explained it. "I'm doing this video so that people who can't come will still be able to see what I'm seeing."

The following day—still 24 hours before the opening and unveiling—Anomaly held an in-store media event to spark coverage and conversation, and of course to stimulate day one sales. In keeping with Lauren's micromaven heritage and the integrity of the By Lauren Luke brand, no traditional mass media outlets were on the invite list. Not a single newspaper, television station, radio news crew, or women's magazine reporter was in the room on the evening of July 30. "We invited 75 or so bloggers and social media people to come, meet Lauren, and learn about her story," said Franke Rodriguez, the Anomaly executive who manages the By Lauren Luke business. But more important, they also extended an open invitation to the community of fans, friends, and potential buyers that had been with Lauren throughout her journey from unknown eBay reseller to burgeoning global microbrand. That evening, the 75 handpicked consumer content creators were joined by more than 500 real women and girls who wanted to share in Lauren's experience and meet the everywoman whose passion, personality, and point of view had come to mean so much to them. During our conversation about the launch event, Franke offered his perspectives on how it worked and what it meant for the brand and its public. As he spoke, his voice betrayed a sense of wonder.

It's funny, because I was pretty skeptical going into it, but after that event ... Greg, I have never been so emotional in my life. We've all seen video of celebrity meet and greets where the fans wait in line and they're crying because they're so overcome with emotion. And you think, "Man, that's so ridiculous." But here I am with this YouTube makeup phenomenon and 500 people show up at Sephora to see her. One girl drove 16 hours from Michigan because Lauren's outlook had touched her in such a way that she absolutely had to meet her in person. This other girl—a 14-year-old from Princeton, New Jersey—skipped school and had a friend's mom bring her into the city because her own mother couldn't get off from work. The line is selling well but this goes beyond being just another makeup business. There's a real person behind it, she cares about her "friends"—she doesn't call them customers or fans or followers, to her they're friends—and she understands what she means to them. And you know, *they mean a lot to her too.*

Without a doubt, most corporations recognize the value of loyal customers—the proverbial 20 percent of buyers who contribute 80 percent of revenue—but it seems few recognize how important it is to demonstrate loyalty *to* customers. In By Lauren Luke, both Anomaly and Lauren herself have always been and are committed to remaining focused on building and being a loyal brand.

On the strength of the New York product line premier, Anomaly and Sephora planned a follow-on series of Lauren Luke promotional appearances at stores across the country in early 2010.[6] While the beauty products retailer routed the tour to stop in major markets throughout the United States—places like Miami, Austin, Phoenix, and Los Angeles, cosmopolitan cities representing high-density pockets of Lauren Luke fans and cosmetics buyers—Luke was predictably more interested in meeting as many friends as possible regardless of where they lived. Rather than simply embark on a high-glitz media tour that hit just a small handful of big cities, Luke and her team chose to traverse the United States in a rented tour bus, stopping off in as many towns as possible to host casual meet and greets. That idea came from Lauren herself and is consistent with her authentic, homegrown, loyal brand persona.

"When Lauren suggested the road trip, I thought, *yeah, of course, that's exactly the right way to do it*," Franke recalls. "It's not just about Sephora visits, the press we generate, and the product we sell. It's about giving your friends an opportunity to join you on the journey. It reinforces the idea that no matter how big and how successful you get, you'll always be one of them. You're just the girl in her bedroom, putting on eye shadow in front of a Webcam."

microMARKETING SUCCESS THROUGH THE SEVEN SHIFTS

By tapping into the power and potential of the social Web and a variety of micromarketing approaches—employed together and in tandem to deliver the desired results—Lauren and her partners at Anomaly have created a global microbrand that is *of our times* and sustainable *over time*. With the first eight chapters in the rearview mirror, I have no doubt that you already recognized a number of these micromarketing principles in action as you read Lauren Luke's story, but let's take a deeper look at the By Lauren Luke case study through the lens of the seven shifts from mass to micro. It will serve to tie together and summarize the key themes presented in Chapters 1 through 8.

From Mass Communications to Masses of Communicators

Lauren Luke herself is a perfect case of *brand as micromaven* and—with her face, voice, sensibility, and steady stream of original content—represents an interesting model for a new breed of micromaven-led organization. With a simple, consumer-grade Webcam and a YouTube account, she reinvented herself as a successful microbroadcaster devoted to sharing her home-taught personal beauty expertise as a means of connecting with potential customers and increasing online sales.

Through a combination of rough-and-ready authenticity, persistence, and consistency in her microcontent output, along with a unique and refreshing point of view that appealed innately to an underserved audience, Lauren became influential within her own microculture and credible to the community that congregated around her. While it may be hard for a midsized to large corporation to manage this feat, it is by no means impossible to identify credible experts within virtually any organization and empower them to become effective and influential microcontent communicators.

In turn, the By Lauren Luke partnership's emphasis on social media outlets over traditional media stalwarts at the prelaunch press event represents a second application of the shift toward masses of communicators, while Lauren's insistence on inviting the actual members of her community to take part truly plays into the notion that in the microcontent era we should view all consumers as micromedia outlets and potential salespeople poised to share relevant and resonant brand stories with their own online audiences—family, friends, and even networks of socially connected strangers. Providing access to 75 bloggers and approximately 500 consumers established the potential for literally thousands upon thousands of shared photos, shared videos, tweets, Facebook and MySpace status updates, and dozens of more in-depth blog posts recounting the in-store experience and advocating store visits and product purchases. Over the longer term, the U.S. road tour served to multiply the effect by turning regional micro-mavens into By Lauren Luke enthusiasts and empowering existing enthusiasts—the online fans that made her videos popular and her business possible—to evangelize the brand in new ways.

From Media Networks to the Network Effect

When an offbeat and rather lengthy* makeup tutorial video featuring a somewhat nondescript woman seated before a simple consumer-grade Webcam attracts several hundred thousand views within a one-week period, it is pretty obvious that the network effect has taken hold. Unlike the examples we explored in Chapter 4—MadV, #blamedrewscancer, and Truvia's My Sweetest Moment, all of which put their constituents' faces, voices, opinions, and ideas at the heart of strategies designed to maximize the dissemination of microcontent into the social stream—Lauren Luke herself has remained a central focus of her own content. But it would be a mistake to assume that the microcontent the makeup micromaven creates—itself interesting enough to garner a certain amount of person-to-person distribution—offers its intended audience no opportunity for self-expression and no motive for pass-along.

Luke's distinct underlying message centered on a more authentic, accepting, and ultimately empowering take on beauty—when *favorited, liked, shared, linked, commented upon,* or *tweeted*—provides her audience with a means of letting their personal networks know that they share a similar sensibility and

---

* By microcontent standards and YouTube conventions.

support a shift in how the fashion industry portrays beauty. This in turn serves as its own intrinsic reward or motivation: the sense of belonging to a distinct microculture that believes in, supports, and evangelizes change, a population of women who prefer not to see themselves through big beauty's distorted lens and want to help other women see themselves in a better light. Programming *panacea81** microcontent into the stream gives these women (and often girls) social currency within circles of like-minded individuals, but even more important, allows them to take part in something bigger than themselves.

From Interruption to Interactions

From the first e-mail response Lauren sent to a stranger looking for advice on re-creating the look in one of her eBay product photographs, human-to-human interactivity has served as one of the basic building blocks of the By Lauren Luke brand. Where on the one hand her intriguing combination of demonstration and interaction has allowed her to establish a credible voice and put a human face on her business (she is just a regular woman who believes in what she does, knows her products well, and uses them to achieve transformative results that can be had by anybody), on the other hand it has given her an uncanny ability to lend her community a helping hand. In fact, it was Lauren's effort to help some members of her community re-create Leona Lewis's "Bleeding Love" look that became the catalyst for the launch of her own makeup line.

---

* *Panacea81* is the handle Lauren Luke has used online since she first began uploading videos, a handle meant to represent her hope that her Web activities would be a cure-all that would improve her lot in life. The *81* represents her birth year, 1981.

Even seemingly simple gestures like the video Lauren posted two days before her New York launch event, allowing out-of-town fans to vicariously share in the experience—though mediated by time, distance, and YouTube's interface—reinforce By Lauren Luke's culture of interaction, giving far-flung but loyal followers a *kiss on the cheek* (a small but meaningful gift that strengthens the bond between brand and buyer) and serving as a show of thanks and appreciation.

Even today, two-way interactions—and the benefits derived by both the company and its customers—remain core to the By Lauren Luke way of doing business. While the packaging bears Lauren's name, the line itself is shaped (even defined) through input from the community that Lauren has fostered over time. According to Anomaly's Franke Rodriguez, Lauren's relationships with her fans, her interest in their opinions, and her commitment to meaningful interactions with them are fundamental to her success:

> Lauren has been able to keep the attention of the people who have been following her from the beginning because she involves them in every single thing she does. When you watch her videos you'll see that at the end of each she consistently says, "I want your feedback. I want to know what you think." We're developing a high pigment eye shadow kit right now, with 14 custom colors that Lauren suggested. With many of them, she tweets pictures of the shades and asks her fans, "Hey, help me name this new purple eye shadow." And her fans love it because she's not faking it or doing it just so they'll tell their friends how cool it is that Lauren Luke is asking their opinions. She's doing it because

she knows that the people who have been following her since the beginning are the people who will actually buy these products, and she really wants to know what they think. If they don't like something, she's not going to do it. It's that authenticity that makes everything she does stick.

From Prime Time to Real Time

Lauren maintains an active Twitter profile through which she delivers personal, product, company, and promotional updates, and engages members of her community in synchronous conversation. She utilizes video as a medium to field a large and growing volume of follower requests more quickly—not to mention more effectively—than she can through detailed written responses.

However, her real-time weapon of choice has been the face-to-face interaction—most notably the invitation for friends, fans, and followers to attend the New York launch event, as well as the series of stops during the By Lauren Luke 2010 road trip. As useful as technology can be in enabling speed-to-market and rapidity of response, it is important to remember that real-world, in-person interactions can still be among our most powerful, most resonant means of fostering stronger ties between an organization and its public. Further, it offers ample content-creation opportunities for attendees looking to document, remember, relive, and share their moment-in-time experiences.

From Reach to Relationships

It is telling that Lauren—and by association the business bearing her name—consistently uses the term *friends* to describe the people any other company might call *fans, followers, consumers,* or *customers*. The notion of deep, lasting, mutually beneficial relationships is core to the By Lauren Luke culture and infuses every aspect of the business from the products themselves to many of the ways they go to market. With a steadfast emphasis on inter-actions over interruption, a keen interest in what her community of watchers and customers think, a level of responsiveness that underscores a commitment to superserving her core audience, and an emotional resonance that goes deeper than advertising mes-sages allow, Lauren has built and maintained meaningful relation-ships directly with the right few who matter most to her—and who hold the key to her business's ultimate success.

For By Lauren Luke, the right few include the longstanding community of subscribers, fans, and followers who have stood by Lauren herself since the time she was an unknown YouTube content creator and fledgling online beauty products reseller, the people who routinely seek out her latest videos, offer their own feedback about content and cosmetics, and have the greatest propensity to purchase the products. Today for By Lauren Luke—as it had been for panacea81 from the beginning—the right few aren't traditional media or social media influencers but real people. And with the ubiquity of social computing plat-forms, it has never been easier to connect with, engage, and build direct and personal human-to-human relationships between brands and buyers.

From Awareness to Attention

From an alternative approach to product photography for her eBay store to her pioneering use of video demonstrations to both build her following and better respond to that following's thirst for information about cosmetics, Lauren Luke demonstrated a penchant for innovation, for taking an uncommon approach to growing not only her audience but also her business. In an industry in which big brands court the established tastemakers at mainstream magazines and take pains to associate their lines with supermodels and celebrities, she had little choice but to employ content marketing approaches (even if, as an untrained marketer, she didn't quite think of it that way).

It doesn't hurt that Lauren herself is rather unconventional within her industry. Even in the face of similar pushes by bigger brands, Lauren Luke *owns* her niche. And rather than conform to longstanding, accepted industry best practices that might have allowed her to offer something for everyone, she adhered to her own sensibilities and in the process came to represent everything to someone. According to Franke Rodriguez, "Lauren is basically an authentic, true-to-life representation of the Dove Real Beauty campaign. She's the antithesis of an industry that is fixated on unattainable standards—cover girls and models and all of this aspirational beauty. And here comes this girl who doesn't fit that convention." The approach worked and earned her the attention of a sizable and growing audience of admirers.

Her consistent but by no means heavy-handed application of three additional approaches—offering inspiration, encouraging participation, and giving recognition—has allowed her to hold on to the attention she has earned. While the videos themselves inspire active engagement with their *do try this at home* vibe, Lauren's consistent use of calls to interaction (from her openness to suggestions about which looks or techniques to demonstrate in future videos to her routine solicitation of feedback from her community of friends) bring fans of the makeup artist and her company into the loop as participants, giving them countless opportunities to shape the nature of the content that will be created and the products that will be introduced. The responsiveness of By Lauren Luke to the community's requests, suggestions, and other feedback carries an implicit sense of recognition. When Lauren's friends speak, she pays attention to them—and that of course provides powerful motivation for people to stay engaged, pay attention to her, and support the brand with their wallets.

From the One Big Thing to the Right Small Things

Taken one-by-one—one shared microcontent chunk, a single human-scale interaction, a stand-alone New York blogger event, or a lone breathless fan—any of the elements contributing to the By Lauren Luke brand essence might be insignificant and ultimately ineffective. But taken together, the sum total of these small things led to the creation of a new business opportunity, built a viable and competitively differentiated global microbrand, and has driven real results.

As it has since the beginning, YouTube represents By Lauren Luke's social media home base—a single-source repository of the woman's (and the company's) most compelling video content and a virtual meeting place for Lauren's community of friends. With nearly 350,000 subscribers, the panacea81 channel represents a substantial owned media asset. With more than 75 million video views, it provides the brand with a hotbed of earned attention: visitors have posted over 36,000 comments to the channel's home page alone, and any given video can amass hundreds of viewer comments within just a day of its original upload. Lauren herself has attracted roughly 30,000 Twitter followers and 30,000 Facebook fans, and with her personal profiles serving as de facto social network outposts for her company, the business stands to benefit from these additional communities of engaged consumers. In fact, her successful track record in owned media and earned attention has been a key driver of her push into not only mainstream retail, but also mainstream media including her book deal, her QVC slot, a BBC documentary, and an impressive array of print features.

See How Lauren Luke Connects with Her Friends

uk.youtube.com/panacea81

bit.ly/panacea81facebook

twitter.com/panacea81

twitter.com/bylaurenluke

Most of all though, By Lauren Luke has seen tangible, measurable business results—including better-than-expected revenue, of course—predominantly through the use of a micromarketing-based strategy and a series of small but effective micromarketing tactics. "We launched a new brand with no advertising budget, no marketing budget to speak of, and look at our sales and what we've been able to accomplish," said Franke Rodriguez. "It's been more successful than we ever could have expected for year one."

ONE MORE SMALL IDEA ABOUT THE PATHWAY FROM micro TO MASS

As empowering as the microcontent revolution has been for Generation C, I've noticed that the most talented (or maybe just the most ambitious) creators constantly seek bigger audiences and higher-profile platforms, often shooting for exposure or even careers in mainstream media. As transformative as the theory of the long tail is, the truth is few companies want to get stuck at the narrow end of the tail for the long haul. Most hope to gradually work their way up to the fat head of the curve, selling more than the vast majority of their competition. Likewise, just about every business starts small, but many—if not most—dream of one day growing big. Some number of them will of course succeed. When they do, shifting a few units or attracting the attention of just a few customers is no longer enough, and marketing in a way that quite simply cannot deliver massive results is not an option.

So does this mean that micromarketing is an approach best suited to small businesses, underdog challengers, individual strivers, and grassroots organizations? I would hope the answer to this question should be apparent given that I've argued my case and illustrated my points in part with stories of microfueled activations by global giants like Best Buy, Coca-Cola, Ford, Panasonic, and Walmart, among others. But to be clear, the answer is obviously *no*. In fact, the assumption that thinking and acting small will necessarily deliver small results couldn't be farther from the truth.

While micromarketing taps into the power of small things, urges organizations to think and act small, and finds opportunity in harnessing the potential of microcontent to convey brand stories in new ways, the individuals and companies that apply micromarketing's principles are not (and should not be) satisfied with small results. Micromarketing as an approach might favor tweets over television, posts over publications, the stream over the site, and peer-to-peer distribution over the portal destination, but as a business driver, it can be highly effective in engaging massive consumer populations and delivering big results.

In an age when mainstream has all but lost its meaning and traditional media has proved to be increasingly ineffective at reaching the masses, going micro might turn out to be one of the most effective means of achieving even your most aggressive marketing goals and business objectives. I hope you'll seize the opportunity to tap into this bold new reality to get big results for your own business, and I'd like to devote the remainder of this book to helping you get started.

MICRO ME: CONNECT, CONVERSE, AND CONTINUE

Let's face facts: a traditional book (even one you might be reading on a Kindle, Nook, Sony Reader, iPad, or even online) isn't exactly the most micro of media. This book is essentially the work of one communicator rather than the product of collaboration among many; it's not especially interactive; it can't easily be pushed into the social stream; it isn't built to foster real human relationships; and doesn't take particularly well to real-time updates. But hopefully at least a few of the ideas included within this book's pages did earn your attention, and I hope you'll recommend it to your network of connections, colleagues, clients, friends, and (why not) family.

So in an effort to practice what I preach and extend this book beyond the printed page, I would like to suggest a variety of small things you can do to learn more, access supplemental microcontent, get updates on new developments related to the ideas in the book, share your own ideas about micromarketing, connect with me (and one another), and keep the dialogue going even after you've closed the cover:

➡ If it weren't for my blogs, I probably never would have been asked to write this book. So now that you've read the book, you might enjoy the content that I publish regularly on my blogs. Although I write and post on at least four different sites, the two that you're most likely to find interesting and relevant are **www.gregverdino.com** and **www .verdinobytes.com**. On the first, I regularly write about the themes covered in this book along with other social media, marketing, technology, and general business topics. On the second, I simply collect, curate, and share bits of microcontent that I find interesting as I make my way around the Web—it's a great snapshot of what has earned my attention at any given time.

➡ If you're interested in connecting with me personally across the social Web, the best places to start are Twitter and Facebook, where you can find me at **www.twitter .com/gregverdino** and **www.facebook.com/gregverdino**, respectively. However, as a big proponent of practicing what I preach, I am also present on just about every social service I mention throughout this book—Delicious, Flickr, Foursquare, Google Buzz, LinkedIn, Tumblr, and YouTube, among others, although I am not equally active on every service and my platforms of choice often change based on where my friends and colleagues spend their time. I generally use *gregverdino* as my profile name. It's not especially creative, but it works well for personal branding and makes it easy for people to find me.

➥ If all this is too much for you, I am more than happy to strike up a conversation over e-mail. You can reach me at **greg.verdino@powered.com**.

➥ I also understand that, at the end of the day, face-to-face interactions often trump digital connections when it comes time to get some real work done. If you'd like to get some real work done together, I am available for speaking engagements (see **bit.ly/verdinospeaks** for more information), and my company, Powered (**www.powered.com**), is available to help you employ micromarketing principles to get big results for your business today.

➥ Finally, I'd like to remind you that—if you haven't done so already as you were reading along—you can go online to access enhanced content, meet other readers, engage in discussions, share your own micromarketing stories, and get exclusive updates. Visit **www.microMARKETINGbook .com**, join the community of micromarketing readers at **www.facebook.com/micromarketing,** and get real-time updates, new thinking, and links to interesting stories as they develop by following **www.twitter.com/micromktg**.

MICRO YOU: SO WHAT'S *YOUR* STORY?

In the Preface, I expressed my hope that this book would inspire you to challenge your status quo and your time-worn notions about what works, and then I went on to present my own thoughts over the course of more than 200 printed pages. If I did my job properly, you have at least begun to think about marketing in a new way and are considering what micromarketing can mean for you. So before you close the cover and fire up your browser, I'd like to give you the opportunity to really contemplate how you might apply some of the ideas and approaches I've laid out in these first nine chapters to your own marketing goals and business challenges. Grab a pen and turn the page.

10

What Small Things Will You Do Today?

Applying microMARKETING Approaches in Your Business Right Now

"Micromarketers think and act small, because in an era of microcontent and microcultures, the biggest opportunities—and the opportunity to not only survive but *thrive* in the post–mass marketing age—lie not in the one big thing but in lots and lots of small things."

YOUR *THINK SMALL* ACTION PLAN

At this point, I hope I have given you a clear sense of what I mean by micromarketing and how big businesses, scrappy start-ups, and even individuals have applied a *think small* mindset and *act small* approaches to drive meaningful, measurable results. If I've accomplished that much, then I assume you are already considering a variety of ways you can apply what you have learned to your own business and life. I wouldn't expect that you will find a place in your plans to experiment with each and every idea I've presented, but if you can identify even a handful of the right small things for your organization, then you will have taken the first steps toward transforming the way you do business and drive results in the post–mass marketing age. To help you get started, I've structured this final chapter as a series of 40 thought-provoking questions—organized by chapter so you can more easily refer back to the text if you need a refresher, and with ample room for you to jot your notes right on the pages.

Build Your *Think Small* Action Plan Online

If you need additional copies of the questionnaire for yourself, would rather not mark up the book, might like to share it with your business colleagues and online connections, or simply prefer your media digital, you can also access the same material on the *microMARKETING* Website: www.micromarketingbook/thinksmallactionplan.

Thinking About and Acting On the Ideas in Chapter 1

1. Most businesses can identify at least one microculture for which it can supersatisfy hyperniche needs or interests with either products or brand-relevant content. What microcultures can *your* business serve?

_____

_____

_____

_____

_____

_____

_____

2. Think about the content your organization already creates.
    Do you blog, tweet, or create videos, e-books, white papers,
    or other thought leadership? Do you offer interesting or help-
    ful utilities that can be distributed on social platforms?

    _____

    _____

    _____

    _____

    _____

    _____

3. How much of your content is presented on your Website or
    in other macro formats? How could this content be micro-
    chunked so that it could be more easily linked to, syndicated,
    shared in the social stream, remixed, filtered, or tweaked?

    _____

    _____

    _____

    _____

    _____

    _____

4. If you had trouble answering the questions above, what other types of content could your company create (or source) to increase the pool of brand-relevant microcontent assets?

_____

_____

_____

_____

_____

_____

_____

Thinking About and Acting On the Ideas in Chapter 2

5. Has your company identified any consumer enthusiasts or evangelists who are already creating pro-brand content or conversations online or within social networks? Who are they, and what are they doing?

_____

_____

_____

_____

_____

6. If so, have you ever engaged them directly? How? Did you offer them tools, content, recognition, support, etc., and what else might you do to engage them more effectively?

_____

_____

_____

_____

_____

_____

7. If not, how might you go about finding enthusiasts or evangelists? Where would you look, what would you be looking for, and what might you do to establish direct relationships?

_____

_____

_____

_____

_____

_____

8. How comfortable would your organization be to cede some control over message and distribution to consumers? In other words, how likely are you to treat individual customers as collaborators, colleagues, or coconspirators?

_____

_____

_____

_____

_____

_____

_____

9. What are some of the things you could do to encourage and enable consumers to share brand-positive stories about your business or to band together as a community of like-minded supporters for your products or services?

_____

_____

_____

_____

_____

_____

Thinking About and Acting On the Ideas in Chapter 3

10. Has your company identified the micromavens that are already satisfying (with their blog posts, tweets, videos, photos, etc.) the information needs of the microcultures you can serve? If so, list them here. If not, outline your thoughts on how you might go about finding at least a few.

   _____

   _____

   _____

   _____

   _____

   _____

11. Have you ever tapped relevant micromavens to act as ambassadors, evangelists, or salespeople who can directly reach the people you hope to influence or engage? How have you done this in the past? What are some ways you might begin now or improve upon what you've already done?

   _____

   _____

   _____

   _____

   _____

12. What can your organization offer—information, opportunities, access, products, services, etc.—to micromavens to make it worth their while to engage with you directly and share brand stories with their networks? In other words, how can you turn micromavens into enthusiasts?

_____

_____

_____

_____

_____

13. Thinking about the audiences you already aggregate on your Website, at your events, through your media buys, or with traditional marketing, what are some of the ways you can celebrate and elevate microcontent creators who already are (or might, with the right inspiration, be interested in) creating content that supports your existing messaging or value proposition?

_____

_____

_____

_____

_____

14. What types of Web presences could your company create that would curate the best microcontent already being created by others (real people's blog posts, tweets, photos, videos, and more) and then filter, contextualize, and present it in a way that delivers value for your customers and prospects?

_____

_____

_____

_____

_____

_____

Thinking About and Acting On the Ideas in Chapter 4

15. How likely is your existing content to be shared person-to-person in the stream, *as part of the stream rather than as an interruption to its flow*? How could you increase the likelihood that this happens?

_____

_____

_____

_____

_____

_____

16. What kinds of interesting content, utilities, or applications could your company create (other than traditional advertising) that could be seeded by you and would be shared, liked, linked, commented on, tweeted, or acted upon by consumers?

_____

_____

_____

_____

_____

17. When creating content you hope will be shared in the stream, how might you accelerate pass-along by leaving room for consumers to add their own spin, reinterpret or remix your message, and view your content as inspiration to share something about themselves in addition to something about your brand?

_____

_____

_____

_____

_____

18. What are some of the ethical ways you might motivate or incentivize sharing among your core customers, influencers, or tastemakers who act as programmers of their networks' social streams?

_____

_____

_____

_____

_____

_____

Thinking About and Acting On the Ideas in Chapter 5

19. In what ways could human-scale interactions put a human face on your organization and establish experts within your company as credible within the communities you serve today or hope to serve in the future?

_____

_____

_____

_____

_____

_____

20. How can your business lend its customers, prospects, or even consumers in general a helping hand through human-to-human microinteractions? In other words, what unique value do you bring to the table, and how can you share that value in meaningful ways with the communities and micro-cultures you serve?

_____

_____

_____

_____

_____

_____

21. What are some of the ways in which you can kiss your customers on the cheek—surprise them, delight them, express your gratitude in a variety of small ways—in the course of managing the personal interactions between your organization and its public?

_____

_____

_____

_____

_____

_____

22. What are some of the best places to conduct these human-scale microinteractions? Be sure you think beyond Twitter and Facebook; consider how you might find, monitor, and participate in message boards, on forums, in online communities, in the blogosphere, on your own Web properties, in your own physical locations, or at real-world events.

_____

_____

_____

_____

_____

_____

Thinking About and Acting On the Ideas in Chapter 6

23. How real time is your organization today? Does it take you moments to respond to consumer needs, issues, complaints, or opportunities—or does it take you days?

_____

_____

_____

_____

_____

_____

24. What are some of the things you can do to help your organization adopt a real-time–friendly structure, culture, or mindset? In doing so, how can you scale your ability to handle
real-time one-on-one interactions so that they can be
conducted in volume with a consistent standard for both
response time and quality of engagement?

_____

_____

_____

_____

_____

_____

25. Who in your company is best suited to (and most capable of)
conducting real-time interactions directly with consumers?
What departments do they work in, what roles do they fill,
and how many of them work within your organization
today?

_____

_____

_____

_____

_____

_____

26. Where on the social Web do your customers congregate, and what opportunities do these sites, networks, or platforms offer for real-time interactions? How can representatives from your organization participate and add value?

_____

_____

_____

_____

_____

27. Do you feel that you've ever missed out on a business or marketing opportunity because your organization wasn't able to act quickly enough (e.g., to do business at the speed of now)? What are some of the obstacles you will need to tackle to ensure this doesn't happen again next time around?

_____

_____

_____

_____

_____

_____

Thinking About and Acting On the Ideas in Chapter 7

28. Thinking about your customer relationships today, would you characterize them as predominantly exchange-oriented or communal? In other words, do your "relationships" begin and end with the sale, or are you actively striving to establish, maintain, and grow something more meaningful and lasting?

_____

_____

_____

_____

_____

29. What are some of the ways in which your organization can share control with its customers, establish and reinforce its trustworthiness, ensure mutual satisfaction between the company and its customers, and maximize the level of commitment each party feels to maintaining and promoting the relationship it has with the other?

_____

_____

_____

_____

_____

30. How can you identify and engage key customers or prominent influencers (in other words, *the right few*) in communal relationships? What would you offer, and what would you expect in return?

_____

_____

_____

_____

_____

31. What are some of the ways in which you would harness the marketing power of the right few by giving them the means and motivation to serve as ambassadors and evangelize your organization, products, or services to their personal networks and even a larger population of consumers? In other words, *how can you empower your customers to create customers?*

_____

_____

_____

_____

_____

32. How will you measure the strength of your organization-to-public relationships and the effectiveness of these relationships in establishing credibility among a desirable audience, reaching a larger population, and driving consumers to action?

_____

_____

_____

_____

_____

Thinking About and Acting On the Ideas in Chapter 8

33. How effective do you feel your organization has been in earning the attention of your core constituents, particularly through social media?

_____

_____

_____

_____

_____

34. What innovative approaches have you tried, and what are some of the uncommon paths you can follow in order to more effectively earn media and attention? Think about how microcontent, microinteractions, creativity, and unexpected ideas and executions can provide your organization with an advantage.

_____

_____

_____

_____

_____

_____

35. Where can your organization be present, seed content, or offer value in order to increase its likelihood of attracting attention among relevant audiences? What assets (content, utilities, tools, etc.) or resources (financial, human, or otherwise) will you need in order to be effective?

_____

_____

_____

_____

_____

_____

36. What types of impossible-to-ignore interactions can you inspire, and what can you do to increase the likelihood that consumers will become active participants and therefore attentive and highly engaged audiences?

_____

_____

_____

_____

_____

37. What are some of the ways your organization can give attention—offer recognition to your customers, prospects, and enthusiasts, especially when they've chosen to become actively engaged in supporting your micromarketing efforts and evangelizing your company, products, or services to their friends, families, colleagues, and connections?

_____

_____

_____

_____

_____

Thinking About Results

38. Now that you've begun to think through how you can apply micromarketing principles and approaches in your own business, let's think a bit about achieving results. What are some of the business and marketing goals you can achieve by acting on the ideas you outlined above?

_____

_____

_____

_____

_____

_____

39. What are some of the ways the addition of micromarketing approaches to your overarching marketing and communications mix will allow your organization to achieve your goals more effectively or more efficiently, or even accomplish things you have been unable to do with more traditional approaches?

_____

_____

_____

_____

_____

40. What will you look to as key performance indicators, and
how will you measure your success against them?

_____

_____

_____

_____

_____

_____

_____

As you've gone through the process, I hope you have gleaned
at least a few insights, identified a variety of different ways to
get started with micromarketing, and begun to think through at
least a straw man for an action plan that you can execute against.
On the one hand, you can rest assured that although you are
forging a new path for your own organization, in this book
I have given you a number of viable ideas and approaches and
illustrated how a number of other organizations—not to mention
individuals—have already traveled the road before you. I would
encourage you to seek out your peers and connect with innovative individuals who seem to be getting it right. I invite you to
start a conversation with me and remain in touch as you and
I both continue to think through how businesses can find

opportunity in the shift from mass to micro. And I hope you will share the lessons you learn through your own successes—and just as important, your failures—with both your colleagues and your network of connections as you discover what is working well for you. But most of all, I wish you all the best and your company the biggest results.

Endnotes

CHAPTER 1

1. bit.ly/atlantic-livetweetingtherevolution
2. bit.ly/formerly-the-audience
3. bubblegeneration.com/2005/11/media-2.cfm
4. bit.ly/smallpieces

CHAPTER 2

1. bit.ly/paranormal-timesonline
2. eventful.com
3. eventful.com/demand
4. bit.ly/paranormal-seattlepi
5. bit.ly/paranormal-mmm
6. bit.ly/paranormal-cbs
7. mashable.com/2009/10/13/paranormal-activity-success
8. eepybird.com
9. bit.ly/coke-eepy-wsj
10. bit.ly/israel-massmicro

CHAPTER 3

1. farisyakob.typepad.com/
2. bit.ly/mediationgeneration
3. trendwatching.com/trends/generation_c.htm
4. rocketboom.com/tag/steve-garfield/
5. ireport.com/people/stevegarfiel
6. twitter.com/natasha
7. sapientnitro.com.au/work/best-job-in-the-world/
8. www.mumbrella.com.au
9. blog.sapha.com/?p = 51
10. blog.sapha.com/?p = 51
11. www.steverubel.com/the-next-big-trend-its-all-about-curation

CHAPTER 4

1. frozenpeafund.com/
2. blamecancer.org or getsatisfaction.com/blamecancer
3. socialvibe.com
4. buzzmachine.com/2009/11/30/media-after-the-site
5. bit.ly/lifestreams
6. danah.org/papers/talks/web2expo.html
7. bit.ly/adweek-truvia

CHAPTER 5

1. zachbraiker.com
2. well.com
3. rheingold.com
4. brightkite.com
5. foursquare.com
6. gowalla.com
7. mashable.com/2009/12/23/pepsi-super-bowl/
8. bit.ly/tns-ad-decline
9. bit.ly/theyearmarketingdies
10. fredmiranda.com
11. dpreview.com
12. nikonians.org
13. zappos.com

CHAPTER 6

1. revision3.com
2. en.wikipedia.org/wiki/prosumer#producer_and_consumer
3. bbyconnect.appspot.com
4. yammer.com

5. twitter.com/bjmendelson
6. soapboxincluded.com/2009/09/15/twelpforce-is-on-the-way
7. marshallk.com
8. http://bit.ly/rww-realtime
9. skypejournal.com
10. twitter.com/evanwolf
11. bit.ly/rww-realtime-comment
12. oneriot.com
13. topsy.com
14. collecta.com
15. yelp.com
16. urbanspoon.com
17. flixster.com
18. justbought.it
19. blippy.com
20. delicious.com
21. en.wikipedia.org/wiki/instant-on
22. flipthefunnelnow.com/tim-mcintyres-response-to-dominos

CHAPTER 7

1. dashes.com/anil/2009/12/life-on-the-list.html
2. dashes.com/anil/2010/01/nobody-has-a-million-twitter-followers.html
3. en.wikipedia.org/wiki/Relationship_marketing
4. James E. Grunig and Linda Childers, *Guidelines for Measuring Relationships in Public Relations*, Institute for Public Relations Commission on PR Measurement and Evaluation, Gainesville, FL, 1999
5. bit.ly/bweek-walmart
6. bit.ly/forbes-walmart
7. checkoutblog.com
8. bit.ly/social-walmart
9. couponcravings.com/2008/09/walmarts-elevenmomscom-launches.html
10. nielsen-online.com/pr/pr_090507_3.pdf
11. skimbacolifestyle.com
12. momadvice.com
13. blogtalkradio.com
14. getssatisfaction.com
15. goingsocialnow.com
16. slideshare.net/shivsingh/social-influence-marketing-trends

CHAPTER 8

1. bit.ly/delta-youtube-star
2. bit.ly/reddit-samsung
3. continuouspartialattention.com
4. jchutchins.net

CHAPTER 9

1. gapingvoid.com
2. stormhoek.com
3. gapingvoid.com/2005/10/11/the-global-microbrand-rant/
4. bit.ly/marketingvox-reflect
5. anomaly.com
6. bylaurenluke.com/party.aspx

Index

251

About the Author

© 2010 David Beyda Studio, NYC

Greg Verdino is vice president of strategy and solutions at Powered, a full-service social media agency. He joined Powered through its acquisition of crayon, the strategic consultancy in which he was a principal and at which he served as chief strategist. Previously, Verdino held leadership roles at a number of advertising, marketing, digital media, and technology companies, including Digitas, ROO.tv, Akamai Technologies, Arbitron, and Blau Marketing Technologies. Over the course of his 20-year career, he has helped clients such as American Airlines, American Express, BIC, Coca-Cola, Ford, General Motors, Panasonic and many others evolve their marketing strategies to take advantage of disruptive changes in media, technology, and consumer culture.

Verdino writes a popular and influential marketing blog (www.gregverdino.com), is a frequent conference speaker, and has been profiled in and quoted by a wide variety of news and business media including *Advertising Age, Adweek, BusinessWeek, Forbes,* the *New York Times, Newsday,* and the *Wall Street Journal.* He grew up on Long Island, is a graduate of Wesleyan University, and currently lives in Huntington, NY.

MATTERS

Wouldn't it be great to win big by acting small?

powered thinks so.

We're a dedicated social media agency. Find out how we can make small efforts pay big.

www.powered.com